Herald Express

G000093193

Walking

"With a Tired Terrier"

In and Around

Torbay

Brian Carter

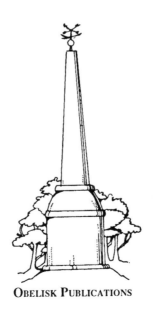

OBELISK PUBLICATIONS

OTHER OBELISK PUBLICATIONS

Places
Around & About the Haldon Hills, Chips Barber
The Lost City of Exeter, Chips Barber
The Torbay Book, Chips Barber
The Great Little Dartmoor Book, Chips Barber
The Great Little Exeter Book, Chips Barber
Made in Devon, Chips Barber & David FitzGerald
Dartmoor in Colour, Chips Barber
Burgh Island & Bigbury Bay, Chips Barber & Judy Chard
Exeter in Colour, Chips Barber
Torbay in Colour, Chips Barber

Walking
Diary of a Dartmoor Walker, Chips Barber
Adventure Through Red Devon, R. B. Cattell
Under Sail Through South Devon and Dartmoor, R. B. Cattell
Diary of a Devonshire Walker, Chips Barber
Rambling in the Plymouth Countryside, Woolley & Lister
The DevonAir Book of Family Walks, Chips Barber
Running in Devon, John Legge

Spooky
Tales of the Unexplained in Devon, Judy Chard
Haunted Happenings in Devon, Judy Chard
Dark & Dastardly Dartmoor, Sally & Chips Barber
The Ghosts of Exeter, Chips Barber
The Ghosts of Torbay, Deryck Seymour

Nostalgia
An Exeter Boyhood, Frank Retter
Ide, Bill Rowland
Memories of Newton Abbot, Elsie Townsend
Talking About Topsham, Sara Vernon

Old Pictures
Albert Labbett's Crediton Collection
An Alphington Album, P. Aplin & J. Gaskell
Peter Tully's Pictures of Paignton
The Dawlish Collection, Bernard Chapman
The Totnes Collection, Bill Bennett

All drawings and maps by the author
Cover photograph by Chips Barber

First published in 1990 by
Obelisk Publications, 2 Church Hill, Pinhoe, Exeter, Devon
Designed by Chips & Typeset by Sally Barber
Printed in Great Britain by
Penwell Ltd, Parkwood, Callington, Cornwall

©1990 Brian Carter
All Rights Reserved

INTRODUCTION—Why Walking With a Tired Terrier?

Well, I have a ten-year-old rough-haired Jack Russell called Jamie whose enthusiasm for country walks isn't matched by his stamina. So, when we tackle some of the wilderness routes I usually end up carrying him on the last stretch.

When he wants a lift he just flops down and waits to be picked up. He's getting on a bit and his short legs weren't designed for long, hard treks.

Throughout my life I've done a lot of high mileage walks, in the hills and mountains of Britain and scores of attractive country pub crawls. But Jamie isn't equipped physically to cross mountains or highland glens or deep Welsh valleys.

He loves a trot and an amble so he persuaded me to have a close look at my home ground, Torbay, for routes with which he could cope. He claimed it wasn't dignified to keel over on the hearth rug after a wilderness hike, completely shattered.

Sharing a house with five cats hasn't done much for his ego. The three toms tend to take the mickey out of him most of the time especially when the doorbell panics him out of sleep or when my wife drops a saucepan on the kitchen floor and he hits the ceiling.

I've seen the cats helpless with laughter as the old terrier nods off and falls asleep with his nose in his food bowl.

Before anyone writes in about him fouling footpaths let me assure them that he leaves his card on my property and rarely misbehaves in public. When he does I have the equipment to remove it.

Jamie is a sociable mutt. He likes pubs with big open fires where he can relax and steam after a day in the open air. As I'm also pubby he has had a comprehensive apprenticeship in the art of enjoying inns.

One of his favourite routes is the Clennon Valley Nature Reserve. Here he will sit and watch the dragonflies whizzing and clicking across the ponds while the ducks come and go. But despite his dreamy look he is a Jack and a member of a gutsy breed. Yet there is always humour in his eyes especially when he is trotting along beside me on his lead darting the occasional upward glance.

In the past I've written extensively about walking on Dartmoor and the South Devon coastal footpath from Berry Head to Prawle Point and I've logged my wanderings through the South Devon lanes but I've neglected the public footpaths in and around Torbay—and there are loads of them tucked away in the most unexpected places. Maybe you'll agree that more than a few are perfect family walks, ideal exercise on a Saturday afternoon or Sunday morning.

Walking with a Tired Terrier will give you the chance to explore unknown Torquay taking green paths across green places which are rarely out of sight of the sea.

After hearing that Marldon's Westerland Valley wasn't going to be sacrificed to the new ring road I thought we'd kick off there and take a stroll through countryside that hasn't changed a great deal for decades. In fact I walked it for the first time as a kid backalong with my old man and a dog called Scrumpy. However, at the time of going to print, Westerland Valley is again threatened by development.

Walk 1—Westerland Valley, Marldon

Distance: just under two and a half miles by this route.

The morning had some of April's chill and a hint of rain behind the greyness. June was here but had forgotten how to flame. The terrier sniffed the air as we got in the car.

It was 6.30 A.M. and most self-respecting Jack Russells were still asleep. I parked near the top of Ramshill Road. In the back window of a nearby van the sticker read: "SUPPORT YOUR LOCAL RESCUE GROUP—GET LOST!" It was the sort of slogan a walker and his dog could do without! I put on the rucksack and clipped the lead to Jamie's collar.

Leaving Foxhole estate we turned right into the A3022 Kings Ash Road below Hilltop Nurseries and a short distance from the junction crossed the road into Higher Ramshill Lane where it dived into the countryside at Ramshill Cross.

The hedges were high and bushy and they met in the middle above us to form one of those "tunnels of green gloom" poets love.

But the vandal who dumped the load of newspapers all over the top of the lane probably had less poetry in him than a building brick. Maybe it was a gesture in memory of even greater vandals than himself—celebrities like Attila the Hun and the Mongol hordes.

After only a few yards Jamie and I were conned by the public footpath sign up in the hedge on our right. The stone stile and its stone steps brought us into a field of deep grass which the dog disliked.

Then I discovered it had been a mistake to wear fell-running shoes and tracksuit trousers. Yesterday's rain had drenched South Devon and before long I was wet to the thighs despite hugging the edge of the field.

"What d'you think of it, boy?" I asked Jamie.

"Ruff" he said and we returned to the lane and I wiped him down with his towel which I always carry in the rucksack. Then I wrung out my socks.

The terrier shook his head in disbelief. Why, he wondered, was I wearing such Mickey Mouse footwear?

A bit further on we took the right hand turning at Cruel Cross and were in Leader Lane and the valley under tall wild hedges. Among the flowers in the hedge bottoms were harts tongue ferns and plenty of goose grass.

Me and the dog wandered through the birdsong beneath a big oak as God switched on the sun. It was the time of the dogrose and the hedges were hung with the pinkish-white flowers, small birds darted in and out of them making Jamie jump.

To our left was a field and a brook and black and white cattle on a hillside as green as a Granny Smith. The running water provided that summery English sound which goes with picnics, the shrilling of swifts and Test match cricket on the radio.

A black tom ran along the lane before us and we followed it out of Torbay into the outskirts of Marldon.

Jamie saluted the cat with a bark.

"You're not very sociable, are you?" I said.

"Tuff," he grunted.

Ahead was Lower Westerland with a cream house and rural Edwardian atmosphere. To the right was a giant conifer and some meadows; on the left stood a stone wall which that old firm Moss and Ivy had magicked into a work of art.

Unkempt hedges of hawthorn enclosed the meadows and as we came around the wall at the bend we were confronted by the friendly cream building called The Old Farmhouse. Jamie registered very interesting smells with his nose while I looked over the gate a few yards beyond the house across the barns and byres to fields that arched their backs in the bottom of the sky.

Then we walked the gentle hill between hedges which displayed some lovely adolescent ash trees. To the right was a villa or maybe a couple of villas for the name plate on the wall at the entrance to the drive stated "Westerland Dale" and the ornamental iron gate carried the name "Webber's Nook."

Here I was aware of the valley as an extension of Marldon the community. We were passing Little Westerland to stroll up to Middle Westerland Cross and swing left.

A cock chaffinch stood on the orchard wall and scolded the dog who eyed it with a mixture of irritation and bewilderment because he hadn't done anything. On the other side of the wall a brook no bigger than a trickle ran through a mass of flowering cress and from the roof of the tallest farm outhouse a blackbird sang. Where the buildings ended we were treated to the spectacle of an astonishing hawthorn tree in full blossom.

"Isn't it great," I said.

"Yup," the dog agreed, wagging his stump of a tail.

Middle Westerland played host to a few dwellings and gardens tucked away behind nice untidy hedges. We turned right at the first house and Jamie led me up narrow Westerland Lane past a courtyard and two impressive pillars. On the far one was the white life-size statue of a duck.

Then the houses stopped and small fields began. In the nearest was a huge tree split open and brought down in a storm. From the gateway I could look back over the valley and it was good to see meadows and pastures catching the sun so close to Torbay.

Another of those dark green tunnels of foliage saw us on to the pavement with the traffic beginning to build up on the Berry Pomeroy-Five Lanes Road.

"OK?" I asked the terrier.

"Yup-Yup," he replied gruffly.

So I took his bowl out of my rucksack, filled it with water from the plastic bottle and ate a pasty while he drank.

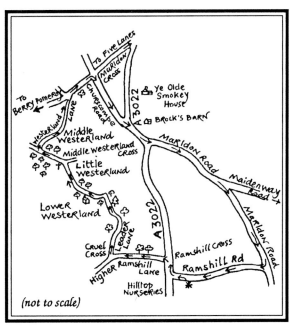

(not to scale)

5

We came back to Ramshill Road this way: At the top of Westerland Lane we turned right and walked to Marldon Cross where we turned right again. Then we followed Churscombe Road down past the holiday camp and came over the A3022 to Marldon Road—which provided pavement walking to the shops and Ramshill Road again.

Walkers who don't mind the rush and noise of nose-to-tail traffic may decide to come directly along the A3022 Kings Ash Road from the bottom of Churscombe Road. This entails crossing that most busy highway twice. The first time opposite Brock's Barn to pick up the trail along the left-hand verge; the second on the brow of the hill where the path ends and switches to the opposite side.

The most pleasant alternative would be to return the way you came seeing Westerland Valley from a new angle.

Finally, this walk in reverse (from the entrance to Westerland Lane off the Berry Pomeroy Road) will bring you into a network of lanes which can be explored using the Ordnance Survey Map 1:25 000 series. From Cruel Cross and the end of Leader Lane swing right into Higher Ramshill Lane and branch left into Middle Ramshill Lane. The return is via Blagdon Lane, taking the second lane to the right at the crossroads to pick up Higher Ramshill Lane and the familiar way back.

Jamie's favourite alternative is to be dropped off at the start of the walk and picked up at the end of it!

Walk 2—Across the fields to Cockington and back

Distance: about four miles.

That Sunday we were out soon after first light and parked the car neatly at the Marldon end of Cockington Road. Then the dog and I came to Five Lanes roundabout and turned right along the A3022.

Jamie paused to snort at a rook that sat on the wooden fence.

"Caw!" the rook cried.

"I bet you said something rude," I frowned and the terrier looked up at me and grinned. Over the sea the sky was blue; over Dartmoor it was grey. The sun shone on us and birds sang as we walked the right-hand verge of the Ring Road keeping to the narrow trail through seeding grasses, sorrel, butter-cups and clover.

Four young rowans stood on the verge, back from the swish and din of the traffic although it was too early for the flow to be a problem, but whenever a vehicle rushed by Jamie flattened his ears to his head.

We ignored the wooden signpost indicating a Public Footpath which simply crossed the meadow back to Cockington Road opposite Occombe House. The one we wanted was green with white lettering that read "Cockington 1.5 miles" despite the efforts of a looby to deface it. This was the beginning of our farmland stroll.

The stone stile provided an easy descent into a field full of buttercups and heifers. A yaffle delivered its manic laugh and received a growl from the terrier.

We resisted the temptation to walk in a direct line from the stile to the gate in the far hedge although there was a faint path. The next field is reached by climbing another stile halfway along the left-hand hedge at the sign.

It was great to be among cattle in Devon grass but I never forget this is farmland and the Country Code must be observed. Yet the irresponsible continually leave gates open and do other daft things. I like to stick to the route, avoid trampling crops and come and go without causing a disturbance.

The young cows pursued us and when one of them lowered her head and mooed at Jamie, the dog took off vertically, transformed by fear into a Terrier Jump-Jet.

More cattle were waiting in the pasture on the other side of the stile.

"Aw-aw," Jamie said but we cut diagonally across the field without incident to a step stile which wasn't marked. Clambering over it we walked alongside the corn, keeping tight to the hedge.

The footpath may take a straight line across the field but I won't go through standing wheat unless there is a definite bold path to follow.

The heat shimmer was making distance wobble, but Jamie couldn't see much except nettles and corn stalks.

"Maybe I ought to get you a set of stilts," I said.

"Huh-huh-huh," he laughed sarcastically.

Torquay was materialising up front to the left and suburban Paignton was away to the right. Stantor Linhay was in the neighbouring meadow on the Paignton side.

A cock pheasant whirred out of the corn hiccuping his alarm. The dog and I exchanged glances and pretended our nerves hadn't been shattered.

Coming around with the curve of the field boundary we were confronted by a gate and a huddle of farm buildings but a few paces to the left of the gate was a gap in the hedge and a flight of steps descending to the path beside Stantor Barton Farm.

Dogs barked but didn't appear as we passed the farmhouse on the right and a vision of Stantor Cottages further up the coombe to our left.

We came along the path but instead of bearing left for the cottages we went through the gate at the bend on to a cart track and straight up over the field to another

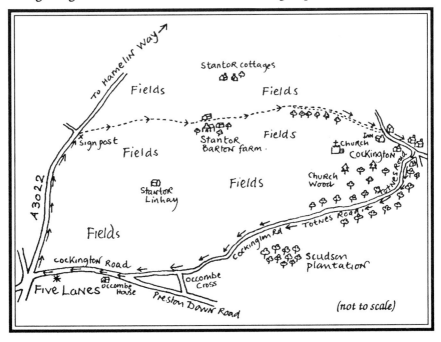

Moo

Larter

gate and another stile. In the meadow beyond I could look towards the gleaming roofs, spires and towers of Torquay and there was a glimpse of the bay which Cockington's trees couldn't completely conceal.

Jamie read the air with his nose.

"Happy?" I said. "Uh-huh," he nodded.

Larks sang, a cock crowed and, with what I presumed to be the bastions of Chelston standing on the hill across the coombe, a cuckoo began to repeat its name. Tight to the hedge we negotiated a funny little metal gate beneath a sycamore and went on to pass through a wooden gate into a muddy land.

Rabbits ran before us and Jamie was alert and quivering. Then he poked his head into the grass and a rabbit shot out from under his nose bowling him over.

"You OK?" I asked.

"Yup," he lied, licking his lips.

On the right were some pines, a row of chestnuts and a view of Cockington Church tower, but Jamie was more interested in the horses grazing the pasture to the left. Behind them was a magnificent hawthorn hedge. Sun, birdsong and all the summer-leafing trees made it a heavenly part of England.

Then we sauntered beneath a quartet of huge beeches with a grey squirrel performing its gymnastics in the fourth.

The terrier was impressed.

The way became wider until rough stony track carried us into the road not far from the Drum Inn.

Putting on an American accent I drawled: "Cockington, Rustic pearl of Torbay."

"Guff," Jamie snuffled snapping his jaws at a fly that kept bouncing off his head. He was referring to my accent not the village!

We walked past the Almshouses and the Inn but with the empty car park to port the old Jack Russell suddenly yanked at his lead. A squirrel was hunting for car-snack leftovers on the tarmac.

Jamie showed his teeth.

"Not a squirrel!" I said in a horrified whisper as if he had just mugged Thumper or bitten Bambi. "Tuff," he growled.

We keep carnivores as pets and expect them to behave like vegetarians.

Ducks were dozing and sunning themselves on top of the wall by the cafe. We tiptoed by and went up the hill to the right at the crossroads. The tourist attractions were shut. The Forge was asleep and it would be another two or three hours before the Weaver's Cottage and Mill Cafe came to life.

The hill climbed on and we went with it past the entrance to Cockington Court, Church and Cafe, although the sign told us they were all waiting somewhere to the right. Yet the parkland spreading in that direction was seductive. Acres of grass and stately trees growing in isolation brought to mind Capability Brown and the novels of Jane Austen.

8

We were walking a most unfamiliar Totnes Road, not THE Totnes Road but a Torbay Totnes Road which led into Cockington Road. I didn't care. A country road is a country road and finding one in the borough is a real bonus.

The uphill going was easy, the way shady, the hedgebanks bright with wild flowers and rooks were mobbing a buzzard in the sky.

The road dipped only to rise again to a hilltop house. Behind its hedges geese bugled and me and the dog were walking out of time across a lost green corner of Torquay.

Up we went through the long low passage of hazels which was rural Cockington Road, small fields on each side. At Occombe Cross we kept right, lured by the bell music of Marldon Church until we met the traffic where the road widened to accommodate Preston Down Road just above Occombe Farm.

The left hand side of the urban Cockington Road offers pavement walking as far as Five Lanes.

At Occombe House Jamie clapped down and yawned from a theatrical sigh.

"You want me to believe you're whacked?" I said. "Uh-nuff," he said. "Nuff. Nuff."

So I carried him the last fifty yards to the car knowing it was a con.

"You old sham," I said and he winked and panted and grinned.

Looking across the road I saw Hay Tor rising above the South Devon farmland from the sort of vague distance I can't resist.

The traffic din at Five Lanes had silenced the bells but most of the walk had been idyllic. It is part of our local heritage which must be handed over unspoilt to future generations

Walk 3—Through Brunel Country

Distance: about three miles

"Isambard Kingdom Brunel," I said to the dog as I brought the car along Moor Lane from Teignmouth Road and turned right to park in the north end of Steps Lane at Steps Cross. We got out.

"One of the greatest Victorian engineers," I continued and Jamie's ears lifted. "The hero of the GWR. He lived in Watcombe. This was his corner of Torquay."

I put on the rucksack and the terrier's apology of a tail quivered. It was a morning of sun and wind, the sleepy side of breakfast. Ahead of us was Watcombe Park which had been open farmland until Brunel planted trees and the man also made banks wherever he built roads.

We came up into Brunel Avenue and turned left to look down on Watcombe and across to Victorian St. Marychurch on the hill.

The terrier tugged at his lead and I let him take me to the gate on the right and the foot-path in the wood. Birds sang, shadows pounced.

We were now on the line of the old coast road that ran up the valley to Stokeinteignhead. Our path of sun-crumbled mud bore to the right with one of Brunel's watergardens buried under a jungle of greenery on the left. Both sides of the track offered magnificent trees. Jamie's ears kept twitching in acknowledgement of some particularly odd bird cry.

To the left woodpeckers had drilled holes in the boughs of the conifers and close by was another jungly water garden. Facing it was parkland of mainly beeches, including some copper.

In the middle of the path were the remains of the brick gully which had carried water down from the top water garden that lay to the right of the bend further up beyond the barbed wire.

It was a mass of rioting plants. "The place has a nice regency feel to it," I said, addressing myself.

But the dog said "Uh-huh," and placed his nose to a twig where a wren had shot its mutes.

Just before the way widened and the red earth held the dance of sun patterns we passed one of the biggest Monkey Puzzles in the county. Now we had a choice of three paths and took the middle one bearing left up the hill.

Through the trees on the right was Brunel Manor, built on the site where Brunel began his own house. Alas, he died when the construction was in its early stages. Yet the parkland is saturated with the man's presence but if you aren't a history buff the glory of the trees is sufficient. The most spectacular is a colossal candelabra of a Monterey Cypress displaying an astonishing upwards sweep of boughs which rise almost from ground level. It was planted in 1850.

We went up a bit of a slope to a path cobbled at the outer edge with limestone pebbles and we walked right, then left at a narrow stepped path to bear right once more on the edge of the wood.

Before long we were turning right into Seymour Drive and well-heeled suburbia. "Maybe you'll pull a posh dog," I said, and Jamie grinned.

Bungalows stood in the remains of the wood at either hand and before us was the pillared entrance of Brunel's vegetable garden. We came to the right of it through the gate and on to a tarmac path. Up to the left was the entrance arch to the stables and our path was signposted, Pedestrian Right of Way.

It led us to a wall of concrete blocks and a bungalow. We ignored the sign on the wall which read: Private Road No Right of Way, for it was directed at cars and motorbikes. The owner is taking it down.

Some domestic geese were grazing in the nearby meadow, but Jamie wanted to greet a couple of Schnauzer pups at the bungalow gate. They were called Bill and Ben, but we never found out the names of the geese.

Presently we reached Teignmouth Road and crossed it carefully into Rock House Lane and a corner of Victorian England that has remained unmolested. The houses are classic examples of Victorian development and architecture on a warm, human scale. Langley Manor is a masterpiece.

The dog and I came down the hill. I was whistling and he was snuffling because a fly had got up his nose.

The walls were beautiful, the hedges leafy and we had fields to the left and a copse on the right and the sea breeze was waiting at Orestone Manor House Hotel.

Just before the bend I lifted Jamie up and we gazed between the trees over farmland to Teignmouth and Dawlish and Lyme Bay. Rock House on the right at the bend was once Rudyard Kipling's residence.

The writer and his wife spent twelve months here, but didn't take to the stuffy business folk of Torquay. All that po-faced provincial respectability must have been depressing.

The steep descent produced another gateway glimpse of countryside and the path was running on to the sea in the tradition of the best South Devon lanes. Alas, the

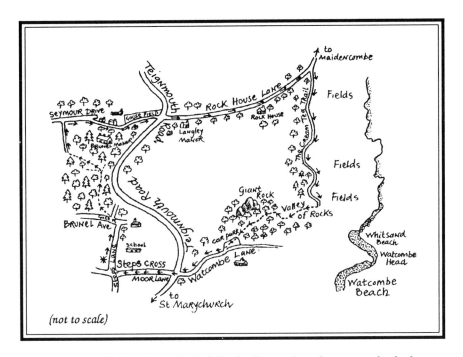

(not to scale)

sea view was blighted by a field full of old cars but there was the hedgerow compensation of dog roses.

On we went past the house called Ferndale to bear right at the bend into a lane marked No Through Road. Then the gateway revealed a miraculous little vision of the English Channel across a field of green barley. It was as Devon as my dad, and sensing my joy the terrier got up on his hind legs and did a dance as he loosed a yarool of delight.

We walked on, me and the brown and white Jack Russell. The hedges were low and tousled, the mud path was grass-hackled and we were treading the Cream Tea Trail.

Throughout the summers between the wars couples took the Sunday afternoon stroll from St. Marychurch along the coast to Maidencombe for cream teas at Rose Cottage. Then, full of strawberries and scones, they walked back.

We came up the hill under the rustle and chirp with the hedges roaring and quaking in the wind. Every now and then there was a glimpse of the sea over waving barley.

It would be sacrilege to take this walk at any other time of the day. It is a morning walk.

Before us were more of Brunel's trees and we strolled into a shadowy dip and up again over dry red mud through the trees to an eyrie on the left that presented a view of the landscape ahead. I could look over the treetops to Orestone and Hope's Nose.

The trail narrowed and crossed the cliff face as the Goat Path which has a handrail and is never intimidating. The sandstone was bright with wild flowers.

Suddenly peeping out of the trees in front of us was the great red dome of Giant

Rock and we were in the Valley of Rocks descending rough steps to a foliage-vaulted gloom. Here the path widened into a sandy ride beneath mature trees. Swinging right with it I looked down on the old clay pits

Jamie stopped to sniff the puddle of feathers where a sparrowhawk had made a kill.

"Ruff," he said.

But we were under South Devon's red Yosemite. Although Giant Rock is partly obscured by trees the majesty of this 150 foot sandstone crag with its overhangs and buttresses is still apparent.

Gleaming in the sun it was an organ crash finale to the wild part of the walk.

A stile dumped us in Watcombe Beach Car Park to saunter up Watcombe Lane with Watcombe Hall to the left and me and terrier alert for whatever surprises the bends concealed.

Teignmouth Road was crossed with similar wariness and we came down Moor Lane past the school to Steps Lane and the car. The walk is one of those rare community assets we cannot afford to lose or spoil.

"You forgot your party piece," I said as Jamie jumped onto the passenger seat. "The old exhaustion bit," I added when he looked up at me from puzzled eyes.

"Wuff," he yawned.

But he was asleep before we reached St. Marychurch.

Walk 4—Green Lanes of Greenaway

Distance: about two and a half miles

The windscreen wipers swept the rain away and the dog looked at me as I cut the engine.

"That Mediterranean weather we had last month has spoiled you," I grinned zipping up my cagoule and clipping on his lead.

We left the car on the hill a little below Greenway Park and came up the road with a blackbird singing in the steady downpour. The old wall on our right was high and wore a toupée of valerian and grass. Then there were hedges on both sides as we passed the railway bridge under a chirp-riddled leafiness.

Raindrops beaded on Jamie's eyebrows and slid down his nose. He walked jauntily in the manner of all Jack Russells and we came by the Galmpton Holiday Park and gone-wild hedges of blackthorn, ash and hazel. A little further on the dog stopped and put his nose to the body of a sparrow.

"Hit by a car," I murmured and he nodded.

A car had also claimed the blackbird lying nearby. The road was surprisingly busy most of the time but we had chosen a quiet Sunday morning and there was little disturbance.

Behind the hedge to the left were the aviaries and pens of exotic birds like silver pheasants and foreign wildfowl and peacocks. The chorus of chirping sparrows meant the pickings from the grain litter were good.

Jamie's ears twitched.

On the other side of the road a metal farm gate presented a rain-blurred view of the Dart but the dog and I didn't linger. The notice board on the tree read: "The Lost and Found Hotel and Restaurant," confirming that this was our route.

At the bend and the second railway bridge we heard the deep throaty puffing of the steam train and along the track come the little green GWR engine making its Paignton to Kingswear run. Steam billowed about us and the dog sneezed. Then the engine whistled and one by one the coaches vanished into Greenaway Tunnel.

"The romance of steam," I said, lifting him up for a look.

"Yup," said the terrier, although he was more interested in the rabbits bolting along the banks.

Bees were tucking into the bindweed bugles in the hedge and a kestrel sat on top of a telegraph pole watched by a family of bullfinches.

We strolled beneath a lovely old oak and a giant conifer. Then there were a line of oaks and a low hedge with another tantalising

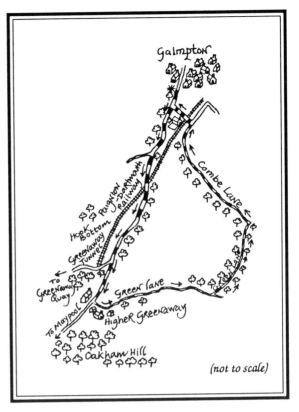

glimpse of the Dart. We were above Hook Bottom at the fork where more advertising for the Lost and Found Hotel was displayed on a tree with Maypool signposted and the road to Greenaway Quay running to the right. (Why is it Greenway on the map? When we were kids we always called it Greenaway.) It didn't matter. We were heading in the Maypool direction, uphill, between low hedges and a free show of wild flowers which would have struck gold at Chelsea.

"Luff-lee," Jamie snuffled, shaking the rain off his head. Moments later he spoke to the pony in the field by the white house but was ignored.

At the second white house called Windy Ridge we turned left and came on by way of the metal gate through Higher Greenaway Farm. The derelict outbuildings saddened me but the horses in the field on the left soon cheered me up. A mare was suckling her foal and Jamie wanted to make friends.

"Don't be daft," I said. "In any case, can't you read?"

The sign by the next gate we had to pass through was clear enough:

"Please close all gates and keep dogs under control"

"Ho hum," Jamie yawned implying that he wasn't the sort of terrier who worried sheep or did anything irresponsible.

Yet another gate had him yawning again but the stony track beyond was delightful. Clumps of clover set his nose working overtime.

At the twin oaks on the edge of the wheatfield we looked down the coombe to the river and Dittisham before rain masked the view; and a moment or so later Jamie had a close up of a weasel. The little mustelid darted out of the wheat in front of him and was lost in the hedge before the dog could react.

The track and the wheat on each side had the feel of open downland about it. Only the larksong was missing but perhaps that was available on sunny days. From here I could look back to Torbay on my right and the Dart curving between the fields on the left.

"From salt water to fresh water," I told the dog. "And all this good green farmland separating the two."

When it's wet it would be unwise to do this walk without rubber boots. It can get a bit sloshy in places. So why not avoid discomfort by wearing wellies as I did. It's not standard rambling gear but who cares. The dog loved wellies and was constantly peeing on mine.

After stepping gingerly through the mud and flood-water to the gate by the old water trough Jamie was sporting red "stockings". With the gate behind us the lane decided to change its character, became narrow and the hedges were suddenly very tall and wild, depositing us in an ash tree twilight where we cut off to the left at the sign which, in fact, suggested we continued straight on. The fox path brought us into Coombe Lane with its fine hedges and mature summer-leafing tree, standing above foxgloves, honeysuckle and bracken. Then we forded a joke of a brook which, judging by the raised stile and wooden handrail to the left, can be a problem for some walkers when it floods.

The lane at this point narrowed drastically and pushed through a jungle of cow parsley. I had to brush the stems aside and Jamie was laughing until he found himself splashing through water and mud up to his belly.

But, to be sure, isn't a little hardship like spice to a walk in such gentle country? Why must we always have it easy? Why must we demand "facilities" and "improvements"? Why can't we meet Nature sometimes on her terms? The terrier did.

"What's it like down there?" I said.

"Ruff uhnuff," he grunted wading along what was now a muddy stream.

But presently the way became easier and a broad stony path took us past the exotic bird breeding centre or whatever it was called. A peacock "eeyawed" and Jamie loosed a gruff bark.

Covered in mud he looked like a real terrier, a tough outdoor type who went and flopped down at the railway bridge! It was pouring now and his eyes were closed as I carried him over the bridge to turn right and clump down the hill to the car.

"Has there been an accident?" a lady called from her Escort.

I told her everything was OK. Then I opened the car and got out the dog's towel and rubbed him down.

"Your act is improving," I said. "You ought to get an Oscar for the Dead Dog performance back there."

"Uhscuh," he smiled, bouncing like a lamb into the passenger seat.

"Want to drive?" I said.

"Nuh," he declined and the rain drummed on the car roof and he settled into a daydream.

14

Walk 5—Along The Orange Way

Distance: two and a half miles

This is another of those short delightful Sunday strolls my gran would have loved.

The car was parked comfortably at the wayside down from Parliament Cottage and its companion.

We had left Totnes Road at Longcombe Cross and come along the Stoke Gabriel road past Longcombe Farm to the Fleet Mill turning where our walk was to begin.

The terrier had slept well and was in a good mood. He walked jauntily ahead of me confident he could handle anything the grey morning might conjure up.

Approached from Longcombe Cross the lane to Fleet Mill is on the right marked No Through Road. The day was very young but a woodpigeon cooed and swallows were already out and about taking their breakfast on the wing.

The privet hedge to the left was flowering and the bank on the other side was a display of wild flowers and cuckoo spit. The cow parsley was taller than me and must have looked like trees to the dog.

The Sabbath calm was ruffled by a surfeit of baa and chirp; but the burnet roses trailing over the hedges were the sort of summery gesture you expect in this part of the world at this time of the year.

"Luff-lee," the dog observed or maybe he was just dislodging a ladybird from his nose with a sneeze.

Before long we had reached a dwelling on the left called The Pound House.

It had a cattle grid and a B and B sign.

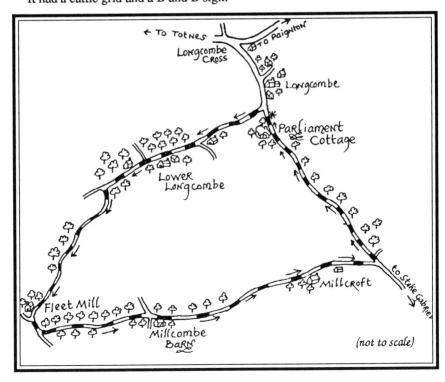

(not to scale)

Then there was a lane of red mud leading into a coombe where a horse cropped the grass. Jamie's ears pricked when a wren opened up in the hedge. The little bird has a song far too loud for its size.

"Hussh," said the terrier wincing.

"You've no ear for birdsong have you?" I said.

"Nup," he agreed.

Weatheracre House in Lower Longcombe turned out to be funny old property a kind of nice gone-wrong Spanish hacienda with wisteria climbing the side of its steps. The farm and old outbuildings were more conventional and in harmony with the landscape. A horse whinneyed from a paddock and was answered by another in the stables.

"Hurrs," Jamie said.

Fledglings were lisping and shrilling from under the eaves of roofs whose tiles wore little badges of lichen and moss. In the corrugated roof of the shed swallows had nested and there was a constant coming and going of adult birds. Beyond the Dutch barn I could look towards small hills and small fields appliqued with brown cows.

At Alex Cottage and the orchard both on the right Jamie met a squirrel-tailed black cat with a lovely disposition and the two animals touched noses. Then we crunched on over gravel and mud between tall hedges into the green half dark of a hazel tunnel.

"Creepy hey?" I said to the dog.

The gurgle of a brook coursed through the hush then we could look down a bank and see the water picking up the light below a hillside terraced with almost perfectly straight cattle creeps.

It was reassuring

carter

It's all Double-Dutch to me ...

to peep between the white bugles of bindweed at a green shoulder of fields with red plough behind it. Reassuring because the seasons were forever renewing themselves and, although I had reached my half century I hadn't tired of dog roses and honeysuckle or the sound of a stream whispering across a summer corner.

We come under a large beech tree into cockcrow which grew louder as we approached a wayside house. The dog and I assumed this was Fleet Mill. Our path was the lane of red mud on the left over the brook. It became stonier as we followed it up the hill towards Aish away from the Dart which was only a field or so down the valley.

"Tuff stuff," the terrier grunted.

"Not for a Canine Commando," I said.

The way was narrow but presented us with a gateway view of sheep pasture on the right near an oak. The ferns growing in the hedge leaned over and nearly met in the middle of the lane. Birds sang but it was too early for the insects to be pests.

The hill become steeper and the rocks bigger, but the yellow foxglove type flower, mullein, in the hedge and an old ash were unexpected rewards. The banks were high and the bracken tall.

Millcombe barn was a living piece of yesterday and the giant oak further on had probably seen the passing of a few centuries. It was splendid, but trees always cheer me up. They stand there advertising the beauty of creation and mutely pleading to us to respect nature.

Up in the field to our right Friesian calves gazed down on us through the hedgerow leaves.

"Wuff," Jamie said. "Wuff."

Suddenly the path widened to a lane with grass in the middle.

"The Mohican Touch," I observed.

"Uhh," he snuffled.

The gate on the right presented a panorama of green fields, coombes and hills which were no more than bumps on the landscape. The house in the foreground of this vision was Millcroft, and beyond a glory of wild roses pigs were rooting about in a meadow. Moments later we passed a byre and came to the Stoke Gabriel road to bear left for Longcombe.

Rooks were in the hayfield cowing and busying themselves amongst the hefty "wheels" of mown grass which lay about like King Kong's toilet rolls.

The wayside hedges and their flowers would make botanists rub their hands with glee. Who needs rarities when the vetch is the most delicious shade of blue imaginable?

I was singing as we came down the hill.

"All things bright and beautiful, All creatures great and small ..."

The larks sounded better but they are at it all day, 11 months of the year. The terrier looked up at me and smiled. He liked my voice but his taste in music is deplorable.

On various occasions over five decades I have looked down from this hill at the grey collection of buildings which is Longcombe. The country road glided between leafy hedges until I was gazing at the weathered thatch of Parliament Cottage. The walls were white and the roses perfumed. A little higher than the wall of the tiny front garden was a grey stone, like a milestone. The lettering on it read:

"William of Orange is said to have held his first Parliament here in November 1688."

I had reached the end of the Orange Way breathing the scent of English flowers beneath the lay of starling nestlings. And once again Jamie had forgotten to collapse.

I didn't remind him as I got out his bowl and filled it with water. The trust, love and gratitude in his eyes touched me.

"Good dog," I said and his bit of a tail wagged.

Walk 6—Clennon Valley—Down Memory Lane

Distance: about two miles

I left the car on the corner of Grange Road, the caravan park side of Cockfosters Inn which, once upon a time, was Grange Court Farm.

Where several roads meet there is an island of grass with the Grange Court Holiday Centre sign prominently displayed.

The dog and I came into Roselands Road (which is a lane) by bearing left at what were once the farmworkers cottages. Then I was walking into my boyhood.

This was my mum and dad's favourite Sunday stroll but the bog on the right and the cidery reek the stream brought from Crabbs Park Winery were gone. In their place were caravans and chalets.

Greenfinches scattered before us into the hedges and Jamie skirted the great puddles which added to the lane's odd wilderness character. It was raining and I wondered how much fine weather we would get in a month noted for its heat.

In 1976 we got temperatures close to 100 degrees Fahrenheit but this morning was very grey and cool. The terrier cleared his throat and splashed on dogfully.

High hedges concealed the caravan park and Jamie was intrigued by the jungles of vegetation where small creatures lurked.

"If a stoat bites you on the nose you'll jump," I said and he gazed up at me.

The lane narrowed and we were pacing along beside a little brook. The coombe on our left was even wilder than it had been in my childhood. Then the brook was gone and we were in the darkest tunnel of brambles blackthorn and hazel I've ever seen. It was like trudging through a pipe.

Before long the dog and I were under the great oak where back in the forties, my dad often stopped to light a cigarette.

Beyond nostalgia's high water mark the way became a lovely stony track climbing between hedges of honeysuckle fern and old ash trees until we were confronted by a metal gate and a stile which dumped us in a meadow of seeding grass and wild flowers. The path was really green here, cutting diagonally to the right with views across the fields to the development of the Fifties on the left and the building of the Seventies on the other side at Penwill Way.

At the hedge we took the right-hand fork and came through the gateway onto the hillside with Clennon Woods before us. Now, although Clennon Hill is marked on the map as a hump in these trees, the dog and I were on my Clennon Hill, the principal hill of my young days. This was the place in my novel *Jack*, where the boy came to be with the horses — Bethlehem, Solomon, Edward and Bathsheba. This was Cider Mill Tor and I have vivid memories of lying in the meadow up there during school holidays just after the war.

I crouched over Jamie and cupped his face in my hands.

"You're a good dog," I said.

"Yuh-yuh," he grunted, stumpy tail a white blur of wagging. "Yuh-huh."

We walked down the hillside into Clennon Nature Reserve between stands of bracken with almost the

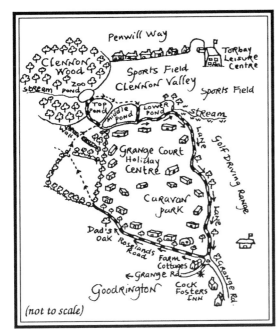

Penwill Way

Clennon Wood

Sports Field

Clennon Valley

Torbay Leisure Centre

Sports Field

stream

zoo pond

Top Pond

Middle Pond

Lower Pond

stream

Golf Driving Range

Grange Court Holiday Centre

Caravan Park

Dad's Oak

Roselands Road

Farm Cottages

←Grange Rd

Goodrington

Cock Fosters Inn

St George Rd

(not to scale)

whole of the valley spread before us — the ponds, the football pitches, the Leisure Centre. But behind my eyes there were visions of yesterday's valley and the water meadows fields of ripening barley, the stream and the linhays.

Behind the hawthorns in the goyal to our right were ranks of mobile homes but Jamie and I were walking through the gap in the stone wall to come slithering down the muddy path. Rain ghosted around us too fine to be a nuisance. The steps cut into the hill brought us onto a gentler slope, past clumps of thistle and meadow sweet, to a wooden gate that opened onto the path beside the ponds. Immediately ahead of us was a swan and her cygnets and nothing in the world would have persuaded Jamie to pass the family.

We bore to the left and a rabbit ran before us showing its white scut. Jamie whined and tugged at his leash.

"OK tough guy," I said. "Fancy your chances with the big daddy swan?"

He didn't and the path led us gently round the edge of Top Pond past bullrushes that looked ready to seed, flowering buddleia and half-drowned scrub willow. Mallard paddled away to hide under the trees and we were on the grass and rabbits were taking cover in Clennon Woods. It was a good foxy place, Reynard's Coney Takeaway, and I was treading across another corner of my past. The grassy level had once been a reed-choked watermeadow where I saw a fox dance. It was up on its hindlegs catching craneflies.

Approaching Middle Pond we witnessed the cob swan's reaction when a rabbit ran too close to the cygnets. He was up, neck arched, wings outspread.

"Hear that big bird hiss," I said to Jamie.

"Huss," he said licking his lips. Then we heard the din of the reedwarblers in the bullrushes at the water's edge. Maybe the presence of four great black-backed gulls on the sports field nearby alarmed the small birds. Black-backs are the gull Mafioso heavies.

Following the wooden pailings of the fence around we walked between Middle and Lower Pond as a cormorant banked and came in to splashdown but changed its mind. At the sluice where the water is taken under the path a mallard duck was fussing over a brood of nine ducklings watched by some leggy young coots.

We walked along the margins of Lower Pond watched by furtive moorhens and before long we found another mallard family, again with nine ducklings each about

19

the size of a bobble on a bird-watcher's woolly hat. Baby birds were everywhere and a libellula dragonfly tacked across the loose strife.

I like the atmosphere of July with its masses of midsummer flowers and hushes broken by the loud song of the wren. A heron left the water and flapped away taking the terrier by surprise. He didn't often meet these Lancaster bombers of the bird world.

"Wow," he said forgetting to put a "bow" in front of it.

I couldn't ignore the fine mature oak on the right in the old field hedge even though an armada of coots and mallard were racing across the pond to greet us.

"The bread hunters of Clennon," I said wishing I'd remembered to bring half a loaf with me.

The three ponds ended at a sluice that fed the stream and its cascades where it flowed between rushes and reeds to the sea at Goodrington South Sands. But the dog and I had taken the lane on the right almost opposite the sluice. In the field above us where the oats were once stocked was a big white folly of a building and the rest of the caravan park.

We walked under banks of bracken and young elms which would never mature because they still had the Dutch disease. A buck rabbit ran ahead of us and Jamie growled. Through gaps in the trees on the left was the golf driving range that had replaced the marsh of rushes, reeds, sallow and willow and 3,500 wild orchids.

The final gate saw us onto the road outside Grange Court Holiday Centre and the path beside it carried us back to Grange Road and the car.

I wiped Jamie down and gave him a biscuit and a drink.

"The old nostalgia trail boy," I said. He nodded, lay down with his legs pointing at the sky and started to snore.

Walk 7—Through Shaldon

Distance: about one mile

After following the Teignmouth Road from Torbay I turned right into Horse Lane a little beyond the filling station and found a parking space against the wall of the Botanical Gardens.

The dog and I were going to walk through the Teignside village of Shaldon and as we set off down the lane the 1950's atmosphere was already apparent.

On the far side of the river a train was clacking into Teignmouth. Another summer day climbed without haste towards noon and gulls soared above the estuary.

Jamie and I swung with the lane past the pink villa called Ness Cottage under an elegant sandstone wall to the right and a ferny bank on the left. The Botanical Gardens were also an the left. They had been laid out and planted with trees from all over the world by a Mr Homeyards—the man who invented Liquofruita cough mixture. His wife donated the gardens to the public in the early 1930s when she lived at Ness Cottage.

The bank and hedge hiding the trees were an unofficial wildflower show, beautiful in itself.

Then the lane dipped sharply and there was the river behind the rooftops of Shaldon. Distances were glazed with misty sunlight but close at hand I was suddenly reminded of one of the reasons why I was taking this walk.

On the door of Stonehaven was a small poster which read: "Hands off the Salty."

The Salty is the tidal island in the middle of the Teign between Shaldon and Teignmouth. Recently it caught the eye of developers who would like to cover it with houses centred on a marina.

But if the charm of this community is essentially 1950s family holiday resort, why unleash the 1980s on it by creating a "boating village" in the middle of the river?

The effect on the water and the marine life would be disastrous and numerous seabirds, wildfowl and waders would be robbed of valuable feeding grounds. The livelihood of fishermen and musselmen would also suffer and traffic increase would be felt on both sides of the river.

A predatory force seems to be prowling the margins of our lives waiting for the chance to move in and change everything in the name of moneymaking.

This force can undermine the right of small communities to control their own affairs, especially if it's backed by central government. What about development

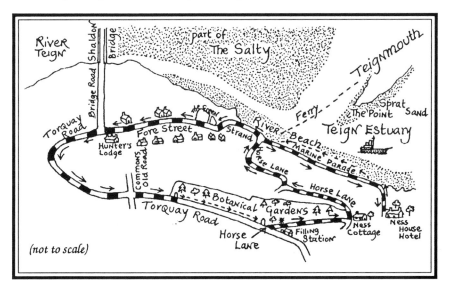

(not to scale)

that favours youngsters born in the town? What about Starter-homes?

Walking down the hill through the outskirts of Shaldon I would have thought the appeal of the place was obvious.

It was somewhere quiet where people could get away from the noise and hassle of the so called "livelier" holiday resorts.

Residents consciously subscribe to this tranquillity and Shaldon remains detached from the frantic rush of modern life. And why not? What's so attractive about bulldozing it into the mainstream of the tourist industry? For every hundred Blackpools and Torbays why can't there be one Shaldon?

Aren't the boat trips across the river, the angling, dinghy sailing, sunbathing and simply being there enough? In blunt commercial terms they pay dividends.

We visit Dartmoor for solitude and wilderness grandeur and would cry out against plans to put a cafe on top of Hay Tor. So why can't the Salty remain the Salty — sand and mud open to the tides, the seasons, seabirds and marine life that favours this sort of environment?

MARINE life not MARINA life.

At the end of the sandstone wall the lane widened to present a view of the estuary with The Point, Spratt Sand, Teignmouth and its pier printed on haze. Gulls yodelled and boats glided by.

The architecture now was typical pre-war seaside—rows of small houses with small porches and all in pastel shades. Almost every window displayed its "Hands off the Salty" Poster

Horse Lane brought me and the dog to Marine Parade. Dinghies lined the shore and holidaymakers sat on sky-blue benches between tubs of flowers. The riverside hotels and guest houses faced the water confidently waiting for nothing to happen. That in itself is marvelously attractive.

The Salty was covered in seabirds and waders were piping on the shore.

White sails caught and held the breeze and the passenger ferry was coming over from Teignmouth. Further along the tideline the fishermen were hauling their seine net but my Jack Russell was more interested in a cocker spaniel called Toby, and Lady and Susy, a couple of springer spaniels that greeted him outside Bay Cottage Hotel.

Their owners came from Tarpley near Chester. Some Shaldon regulars have been visiting the village for 30 or 40 years lured by its resistance to change.

The dog and I walked the road above the shore towards the great wooded bluff of The Ness. Where the coastal footpath began Ness House Hotel provided another estuary view of Teignmouth and Lyme Bay. Returning along River Beach I was treated to little summer cameos.

A schoolgirl loosed her dog for it to splash in the shallows. A group of divers in wet suits boarded an inflatable to go out and inspect a sunken wreck. A child sat talking to a juvenile gull. A lot of quiet happenings were feeding the unruffled atmosphere.

All the holidaymakers, except one, that I spoke to in The Strand and Fore Street were against development on the Salty. Maybe the flower baskets hanging on the front of the buildings were gentle statements of defiance.

The Ferry Boat Inn had a particularly colourful display and a landlord who spoke his mind. Mr Right thought the Salty scheme would be disastrous. A couple of young ladies from Torquay said they were horrified at the prospect.

Jamie and I ambled on past Teign Crest and a side street blessed with fine private houses. The war memorial and bowling green were bounded by rows of cottages but I confess it was the white facade at the London Inn that caught my eye.

Back in Fore Street Jamie strained towards the Royal Standard because he isn't used to passing pubs. "Hands off the Salty" posters were all over the place and it was nice to find one in the porch of the Roman Catholic Church.

We paused at a black and white house standing in its garden with a magnolia tree for company. Then there were lawns behind privet and boats on the lawns.

Rows of sea-sidey houses culminated in the architectural triumph of Hunter's Lodge on the corner of Fore Street and Torquay Road. Dating from 1650 this ranks among the loveliest town houses I have seen. You could get drunk on its beauty and the windows alone would justify its preservation.

The road to the right led to Shaldon Bridge and Teignmouth.

The wooden bridge which once spanned the river was the longest structure of its kind in England all 1,670 feet of it but the terrier and I bore left along Torquay Road into Shaldon's suburbs where fields crept down the hillside to meet villa gardens and parkland.

Beyond Commons Old Road the pavement ended and the road narrowed but no more than a hundred yards further up on the left Jamie and I found a gate in the hedge which opened on to the Botanical Gardens. Lulls in the traffic noise allowed the calls of waders to drift across from the Teign.

Trees and shrubs grew on tilting lawns and terraces of grass. Away from cars and people, Jamie was free to run his nose over things before we climbed a flight of stone steps to a door and the busy road again. The roar of passing vehicles gave the terrier no chance to do his Dying Dog act. It was only a few yards from the door to Horse Lane and the car.

"Fancy some water, boy, or can you wait till we get back and I open a bottle of something stronger?" I said.

"Guh-Nuss," he snuffled, settling on the passenger seat.

"Guinness it shall be," I promised turning the ignition key and heading for home.

Walk 8—Suburbia meets the green belt at Churston

Distance: one and a half miles

Leaving Bascombe Road I parked the car neatly in Green Lane and let the dog out. He looked as eager as I was to walk a classic little route through Churston.

Of course he had to sniff about on the verge and scent-mark with raking hind feet. The villas on the left stood in generous gardens and the fields to the right were small and high-hedged.

Suburbia and green-belt rural dovetailed here under pale morning sunlight and birdsong. Cattle had passed before us leaving pancakes of manure on the road for Jamie to sniff.

At the top of the lane we bore right and came by a beautiful old stone wall to farm buildings with orange lichen on their roof tiles. Young swallows were perched in a group on the telephone wires and sparrows were skirmishing at the wayside for grain litter.

"A barn, swallows, the sabbath calm," I said. "The English summer idyll."

"Luff-lee," the terrier snorted. Ahead, where the lane dropped, we could see an orchard. Opposite Churston Court Farm was the church of St Mary the Virgin but it was too early for the bell music which the romantic in me craved.

At Churston Court Inn we swung left with a tall ivy-clad wall to the right which led us into Churston Road and a right turn that carried us past the tennis courts. A magpie chattered from the hedgerow elderberry and a man on a horse bid us "good day."

Jamie sniffed. He is suspicious of any animal as big as a horse and was still licking his lips to disguise his anxiety when we walked under the old railway bridge into the village of Churston Ferrers.

The row of cottages and their low doors and porches were one of those modest architectural gestures that distinguish rural communities of character. Standing by itself a little further on Myrtle Cottage was another pleasing, unpretentious, building.

And the dog and I liked the row of council houses over to the left. A sleepy cat sat watching the terrier from someone's drive and Jamie, who was raised with five

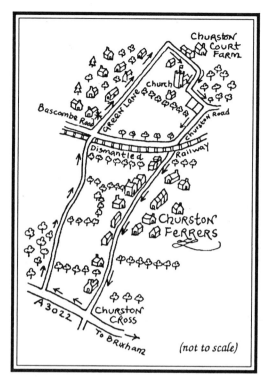

On the map: Churston Court Farm, Church, Churston Court, Bascombe Road, Green Lane, Churston Road, Dismantled Railway, Churston Ferrers, A3022, Churston Cross, To Brixham, *(not to scale)*

cats, wanted to get to know this country tabby but she ran off.

Beyond the warm limestone of a splendid roadside dwelling Ridgeway Cottage with it's salmon pink door stood next to John's Cottage. Across the road was Ferrers Green and we were among some modern development. Churston Village Shoppe was worth the Olde Worlde double "p" and quaint "e". It was part of a little Pre-Raphaelite backwater.

Next door Fir Court could boast a pair of mature silver birches and the open field on the left reminded me of what most of Churston Ferrers was like when I was a kid.

We ambled by West Terrace and its delightful cottages which stood behind small flower gardens drowsy with the buzz of bees.

At Churston Cross we made the abrupt right turn onto the A3022, facing the oncoming traffic which roars along this stretch of the Paignton-Brixham Road. The farmland over the way was mainly under wheat. On our side an astonishing stony stretch of plough carried the eye to an example of modern barn conversion.

"Ruff," Jamie barked at a motorist whose Escort passed at about 80, raising a draught that knocked the terrier off balance.

It was a relief to turn right again this time into Elberry Lane past the sign which reads: "No vehicles Except for Agricultural Access."

A moron with a spray can had defaced the sign but fortunately close at hand was the consolation of a neglected cider apple orchard. The trees stood waist deep in grass and nettles.

Then we were walking a narrow lane under nut bushes and ash trees. A rabbit panicked and blundered through the hedge. The waysides were thick with grass and bracken and a wooden gate guarded the entrance to a field small enough to bring the Forties alive again.

These lovely little meadows lay between the lane and the back gardens of Churston Ferrers and the terrier was dying to romp in them, but dogs and farmland do not go well together and he remained on his lead.

"It's a tough life," I said, soothingly, unwilling to meet his baffled gaze.

"Tuff uh-nuff," he grunted.

The gap in the sky immediately before us had once been a railway bridge, part of the branch line to Brixham which was no longer in use. Stepping under the ghost of that childhood structure, Jamie and I were back in Bascombe Road almost opposite

Green Lane.

The stroll had been so short the dog was taken by surprise.

"Got you," I chuckled and he cocked his leg against the front wheel of the car.

"Canine pee-E?" I said, opening the passenger door. "Or Jack Russell's revenge?"

"Yuss," he snuffled. "Wuff."

Walk 9—Berry Head Country Park

Distance: one mile

Me and the old dog Jamie wanted sea, salt air and lots of sky so where better than Berry Head?

Many of my longer coastal routes begin at the southern redoubt but, lumbered with a tired terrier, something far less demanding was required.

Berry Head Country Park itself was the answer. Nature had designed it perhaps with short-legged creatures in mind.

We began at the car park near the exhibition centre although it was too early to pop in and have a look at the displays Torbay's countryside ranger Nigel Smallbones, had set out. At the entrance to the car park we took the narrow road on the left and made our way past the tame corner of the common with its picnic tables and benches.

Rabbits scattered behind white scuts and the terrier yawned and whined at the same time.

"That makes you look really stupid," I said.

"Tuff," he snorted.

The sunrise glow lit the sky above the sea but middle aged couples were being

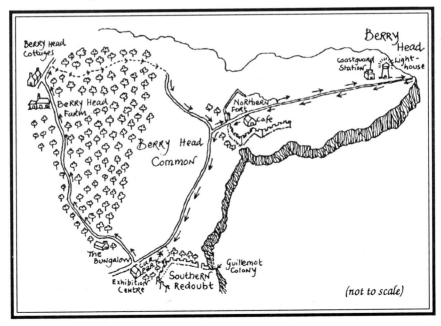

(not to scale)

25

towed over the grass by exercise-hungry dogs. A jogger passed us with lots of wobbly bits in motion and a snarl of determination on his face.

The Smallbones family were still asleep in the bungalow to the left of the road but one of their cockerels began to open up like an alarm clock and Jamie didn't like it. I don't suppose Nigel appreciated it either.

The road was another of those face-lifted lanes you find all over tourist Devon. It had a pleasant rural quality, but I wish it was still a real lane. Red berries were on the hawthorn, the wind was in the leaves and the dog and I were swinging along waiting for Mel Brooks to magic something bizarre out of the quietude. The S-shaped trunk of the sycamore at the passing place had the Brooks' hallmark. Maybe it was a tourist board stage prop.

Where the road dived under a lot of rustle and coo there was a glimpse of Tor Bay between trees. I lifted the dog up so he could share my enjoyment of the walled gardens and orchards. But Berry Head Farm wasn't a farm. It was an example of sympathetic development using local limestone.

Berry Head Cottages, a little further on, were more attractive. They had that Victorian Sabbath calm about them although Mel would have probably sniffed out some sort of Gothic horror given the chance.

Down the hill on the right was the signposted footpath to Berry Head.

"Ruht," Jamie confirmed.

We paused at the wall to look out of the trees towards the sea and Ore Stone and Hope's Nose. No matter what the developers do to the Three Towns the Bay is always there holding the sky as it did when my father and grandfather were young. It remains an area of the past which the present cannot touch.

The path wound upwards through mature trees until its surface became more civilised. A National Trust officer would have applauded this section but he wouldn't have appreciated Nigel Smallbones' tolerance of sycamores. Good old Nigel! He exercised a bit of commonsense and likes to be flexible where the salt-loving maple is concerned.

Emerging from the wood onto the clifftops we were stunned by another pano-ramic view of Tor Bay to the north. Ahead, shafts of sunlight burst from the clouds and hit the sea.

Bearing right Jamie and I walked past the blackthorn scrub and gorse thickets to the path which was signposted Fort Cafe. Here we swung left for the lighthouse, the dog striding out before me pretending he wasn't an OAP.

The cafe was once the Napoleonic fort guardhouse and we were within the ramparts of the northern redoubt. That Bonaparte must have been some bogeyman for people to have built castles all over the place to stop him marching in and pinching kingdoms.

"To the lighthouse," I said, echoing Virginia Woolf. Jamie shook his head.

A yellow telescope beside the cafe gave tourists the chance to look down onto the guillemot colony on the crags below the southern redoubt. But the guillemots' breeding season was over and they were out to sea. A crab boat thrummed by. Gulls cackled then banded together to mob a hovering kestrel.

"Ruff," Jamie observed.

The path eased us further out onto the headland past the coastguard station and the light which is the lowest and highest in the kingdom. The little vegetable garden below it was very Bulldoggy British, proclaiming our genius for thinking small.

Then the head ended and the sky began with the Channel gleaming below us. We sat on the turf and watched ships pass, then we returned the way we had came until we reached the Fort Cafe sign once more.

"Luhft?" Jamie inquired. "You're a living compass," I smiled. And left we went over the common on the path which ushered us into the car park again.

Here the dog keeled over as if he'd been shot

"Why?" I said picking him up. "It's only 30 yards to the car and there's no audience to shower pity on you."

But I guess it was the pro in him. He was a four-legged thespian, a showbizzy mutt craving attention.

A Chihuahua springing out of a posh car gazed longingly at him and Jamie sniggered.

"She's not your type," I said, dropping him to the ground. "Lay off the shorts."

But he was up on his hindlegs dancing and I couldn't help thinking as I opened the car door that it was good to be alive.

Walk 10—Through Paignton Town

Distance: about one mile

Anyone wishing to start this walk from the seaside entrance of Victoria Park as me and the dog did, can put their car in the multi-storey car park next door.

We didn't need the car because Paignton is our home patch and we live ten minutes from the beach.

It was breakfast time and through the windows of Garfield Road's guest houses we could see holidaymakers attacking the traditional fry-ups. The Jack Russell rose on his back legs and sniffed the air. For a moment I thought he was going to croon. "Ah Bisto" or should it have been "Ah bacon?"

The wind was blowing from the west and the morning was cool. To put it bluntly it had been a bloody awful summer.

Crossing Esplanade Road on to Paignton Green at the traffic lights can be a bit dodgy but at that early hour there weren't many cars about. Once he was on the grass Jamie paused and raked away with his hind feet, scent-marking.

He looked like a dog learning a new dance routine. But once he got the smell of the sea in his nostrils he was off with me in tow to walk jauntily along the prom which only needed a brass band to lend it authenticity.

Tor Bay looked about as inviting as yesterday's porridge. It was steel grey, wind ruffled, dour. Three gulls waddled across the pavement to waylay us. They all had colds and were sniffling and sneezing.

"Great adverts for an English Riviera summer," I said and Jamie grinned.

We passed the Festival Theatre and the Crazy Putting course and came to the right hand bend at the end of the green.

Following it around we nipped across Esplanade Road into Sands Road appropriately enough by the Esplanade Hotel. I suppose locals of my generation and my dad's generation will always refer to this strange mock-tudor building as The Hydro, recalling the war years when the yanks were billeted there.

Sands Road is one of the main arteries of my personal nostalgia trip. I used to run barefooted down to the beach over the hot summer pavements back in the Forties when I was a kid. The guest houses with their palm trees and holiday resort names still retail some of that post-war atmosphere.

I lingered at St Andrew's Church recalling mornings when I sang in the choir and had illicit swigs of communion wine. I was paid 7/6d (37.5p) a month for morning and evening services.

On the other side of the road was Queens Park and the athletics track that used to be a coal dump. The new flats further on had replaced the bombed houses of childhood and the lawn at the bottom of Whitstone Road was an improvement on the large house which had taken a direct hit from a German aircraft during Hitler's War.

Over the level crossing we went. An hour or so later we could have stood at the barrier watching the steam train go by on its way to Kingswear.

"Stuhm," Jamie snorted, recalling a recent train ride on this line.

On our right we passed Station Lane, a part of Paignton central to my novel, *Jack*, about a local lad, his horse and the First World War. This was where Chancellors' work horses were stabled. As a boy I often looked in on the Co-op stud and my father

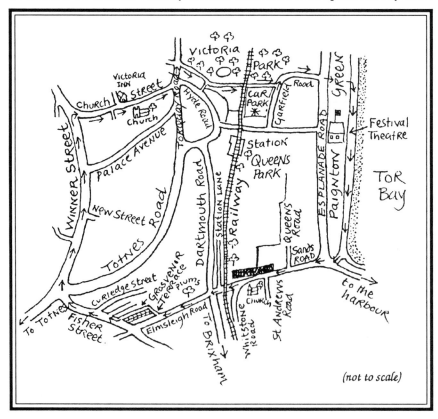

(not to scale)

before me haunted the stables of Torbay Mill and other firms.

Then we went over Dartmouth Road and up Elmsleigh Road. Alas, the plum tree which grew in the first garden on the right, is gone. This yielded the most succulent Victorias I've ever scrumped. They were amazing purple bombs loaded with juice.

The dog and I ambled by guest houses and old folks' homes which had been private houses a few decades ago. There was not a back garden in this neighbourhood that I hadn't visited as a child to scrump goosegogs, plums, apples and pears.

Rather than continue up the last stretch to the crossroads and Fisher Street I turned right in the lane and went straight up over the flight of stone steps into Grosvenor Terrace. This is the row of Victorian brick houses where I grew up. My mam still lives there but the lovely old cobbles have been replaced by grey flagstones.

Well and weren't the little ghosts of yesterday's tackers, tearaways and guttersnipes plotting mischief on the front doorsteps? And wasn't my old cat Nibs going to the lav in Mr Burt's flower bed? And weren't the jute sash cord skipping ropes smacking out the beat above the chanted rhymes? And wasn't my dad ricocheting off the walls as he hurtled homeward after sinking a half gallon before tea?

I turned right at the top of the terrace and came past the gates of Tower House School.

The Marist Convent was no more and the nuns were gone but the spirit of the place survived in Tower House School.

Emotion was subsiding as the dog and I passed Grosvenor Road and Eaton Place with its Dickensian thatch. The old farm, a little further along, had been replaced by some nice modern housing development entirely suited to the area.

Then we were level with Curledge Street and memories of the years I spent in the grey primary school flooded back. The school was still there but Dawes Mineral Works had gone, although the firm is operating successfully from new premises.

I turned up Fisher Street with the past tugging at my innards. The traffic lights were in my favour so Jamie and I could stroll over Totnes Road and on along Winner Street.

The old gossip market was loud with its own life. The family businesses and shops possessed a raw vitality that was totally Victorian. Indeed it is a street full of character and characters, a stretch of noise, jammed pavements and traffic chaos where you can buy a lavatory seat, a lolly, a Chinese takeaway and a second hand book without walking more than 50 yards.

We came past Clifton Road, New Street and Palace Avenue and the three pet shops which have inspired local wags to re-christen the street Winalot Street. At the triangular flower bed that divides the top of Church Street we bore right after a brief chat with Leon at The Pocket Book Shop.

Church Street is another of those friendly shopping areas and as the dog and I paused in front of The Victoria Hotel, a friendly little pub, we got a good morning from Martin the landlord.

Church buffs shouldn't ignore the Parish Church and its fine sandstone tower but I've been in and out of the graveyard for years so I have an excuse for striding on. Paignton Hospital was to the right and the pavement on the left brought us beyond Mr Punch's Bookshop to the traffic lights and Torquay Road.,

Using the pedestrian crossing we negotiated this traffic-bound section and came left on the other side by the newsagents to enter the park opposite the Natural Break Restaurant.

Jamie breathed a sigh of relief. He loves park strolls and bounded along beside the hockey pitch to the tennis courts and the stream. Ducks were on the water and kids were on the swings and a couple of blokes who had obviously been on the beer all night lay snoring on the grass by the pond.

The other side of the railway bridge produced an encounter with the grey squirrels that hang about waiting to be fed. Jamie gazed at the little creatures thoughtfully and wagged his stump of a tail.

We continued our walk alongside the final part of the stream to the Garfield Road exit. Here the water runs on to the sea underground but we were back at our starting point and once more Jamie had forgotten to feign weariness.

Walk 11—Coffinswell & Daccombe—A delightful doddle

Distance: two and three-quarter miles

The car was parked beside the road at Coffinswell just up from The Linny and I took the dog past the pub in the direction of Daccombe. Court Barton Farm Cottage was Devon pink on the left opposite the dereliction which had once been the farm outbuildings.

High hedges stood each side of the road. They were unkempt and a pleasant surprise so close to Torbay. The church was hidden on our right but it could be reached by the narrow path beyond a black iron gate.

The terrier led me downhill now into countryside which developers drool over. May the Lord protect it! Over the hedge I glimpsed fields recently shorn by the the combine harvester. A few decades ago I came this way on my bike to see sunlight gleaming on stubble and stooked corn.

The high hedge banks to the right were crowned with mature hazels but the long downward sweep of road led the eye and the heart into the sort of scene we can no longer take for granted on the edge of The Three Towns. Rural Barton up on the right will soon be lost to houses and a hypermarket.

Halfway down the hill we met Roy Patterson jogging with little son Jamie, and three greyhounds on leashes. Jamie the Jack Russell barked a hello to Jamie (the boy) and we went our separate ways. For a moment or so the dog and I had a roadside stream for company but it soon vanished down a drain.

Sheep pasture ran up against the red sandstone wall of Aynells Farm which, according to the name plate, is now New Aller Brook House. From the entrance to the courtyard I could see guinea fowl scratching around with free range hens and there were ducks in the orchard.

Around the next bend and the gentle climb was a glimpse of Daccombe's rooftops. Again I experienced a curious sensation, something between unease and excitement. It was a feeling I often got as a child when confronted by an unknown landscape. Maybe today it is the result of worrying about familiar countryside in the present climate of land loss.

On the horizon to the right was the dark reef of Lower Killpark Plantation. Horses grazed in the nearby field and house martins were swooping and swerving above a bungalow with double glazing and a garden full of roses. Jade Cottage, with its little pointed porch, was next to modernised Wayside and its swimming pool.

The rise carried us through the smell of farm animals to the white house of Home Farm and the yard and busy bird tables. A bit further on was a rural dream cottage called Apple Acre standing under thatch opposite an orchard of cider apple trees. The pink wash and dark thatch of Combe End waited behind roses at Daccombe Cross like a traditional welcome to South Devon.

"Grrrate," the dog observed gruffly. A wasp sailed around his head teasing him but Jamie didn't bite. He knew all about the buzz that stings.

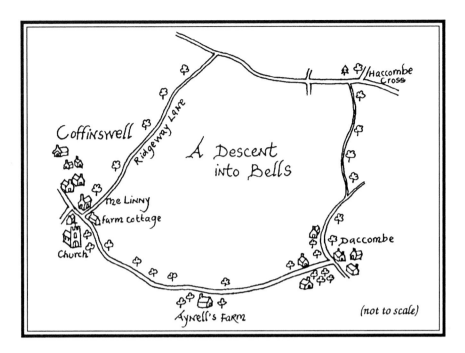

(not to scale)

We bore left in the direction of Stokeinteignhead and Teignmouth. Behind us a buzzard was being attacked by a solitary crow above the thatch and a great congregation of house martins filled the lower part of the sky.

The countryside kept producing little Samuel Palmer studies of rural life—sheep in an orchard, a grey squirrel running ahead of us, flower gardens. Foreign birds sang out from an aviary behind the hedge and I chuckled at the thought of some ardent twitcher trying to fit a British bird to those unfamiliar calls.

Beyond The Old Barn there were more horses in a field but the left-hand fork brought us up a steep hill. The way was narrow and the hedge tall and leafy. Green hazel nuts lay in the lane. Perhaps an elderly lady or gentleman accompanied by an elderly dog might prefer to walk the entire route in reverse to avoid this climb.

At Haccombe Cross we swung left and heard the bells of Coffinswell Church. The road carried a little early morning traffic and seemed quite wide after the hill. We intended turning left again at the top of Ridgeway Lane but there were goats on the road up ahead so we went after them and drove them back through the hedge before returning to Ridgeway Lane.

The view across the coombes and hills to Dartmoor was splendid. Detail was sharply defined in the clarity which preceeds rain. The dog and I marched down into the bell music of Coffinswell with a glimpse of Tor Bay over the fields to the left. The hedges were crowded with late summer flowers—scabious, campion, toadflax and honeysuckle.

The stalks of dead hogweed hackled the hedge top, or were they the legs of sleeping herons pointing at the sky?

The dog refused to speculate. He was more interested in the incessant barking that rose from the local kennels.

"Summoned by bells" we were content to let the country road ease us down into Coffinswell again at the back of The Linny where the tired terrier pleaded to be carried the short distance to the car.

Walk 12—A Search for Sea Dogs

Distance: about one mile

Of Torbay's Three Towns, Brixham has managed more than its neighbours to preserve much of its character and individuality.

It is still the sea port and the fishing village, still the "Mother of Trawl Fishery" and while the glory of the days of the trawlers with their red-brown sails may have gone, the place is still sure of its identity.

"Maybe we'll bump into a few sea dogs," I told the Jack Russell as we ambled away from the car in New Road, the Paignton side of the Christian Science Society Church. We passed the Golden Lion—the town's first and last pub and a procession of little hotels and guests houses, including Woodvale which has a front garden full of miniature Walt Disney characters.

Among the palms were occasional glimpses of Brixham maritime past—fishermen's cottages lost in rows of larger town houses. Brixham's Theatre stood shoulder to shoulder with Brixham Market and a Victorian facade guarded by a couple of modern phone boxes. The Bolton at Bolton Cross was asleep along with most of the town.

The dog and I swung into Market Street and halted in front of Scala Hall where I spent some of my adolescent Saturday nights bopping out the booze.

At the bend on the right the Baptist Church possessed the dignity of a pre-war

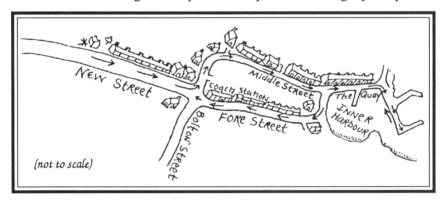

Sunday. The library was across the road and the tower of Lower Brixham church peeped over the rooftops above. It brought to mind the Rev Henry Francis Lyte. Mortally ill he gave his last sermon and sat down at sunset to write Abide With Me. Two months later he died of consumption in Nice on the Riviera coast.

Sea dogs were conspicuously absent. Perhaps a Saturday night of Yo-ho-ho, Fosters and Rum had confined them to their hammocks. It was early and the gulls and pigeons had the streets to themselves, but I enjoy walking through a town or village before breakfast. Traffic is often distracting. When a community is sleeping you can pace around the nooks and backwaters undisturbed.

The Smuggler's Haunt Hotel beckoned from one of these nooks. It stood at the junction of Church Hill West and East in the sort of narrows that must have rang to the clink of the ferule on the end of many a sea dog's wooden leg. This was pirate territory where gentlemen with bushy beards, gold ear rings, eye patches and parrot droppings on their shoulders could cut throats without exciting too much comment.

The bus station opposite wasn't quite so romantic. Jamie and I walked up Middle Street past the coach station and car park. On the left Apters Hill led to the delightful little Manor Inn and views of houses terraced haphazardly on hillsides of the coombe that led to the sea.

Suddenly we were among shops devoted to dispensing ice cream, souvenirs and seaside wot-nots, descending through the yodelling chorus of resident gulls to The Quay. Ahead was the British Fisheries Museum and a lot of Sixties tourist development.

The Rising Sun faced the old fish market whose flower baskets might have inspired a colourful response from the old school of trawlermen. The inner harbour was flat calm which seemed to suit the replica of the Golden Hind at her moorings within easy reach of holidaymakers. Over the road was Brixham Aquarium, an amusement arcade, restaurants, cafes and Pelosi's Ice Cream Parlour. The William Prince of Orange stone on the quay had a spike on the top, presumably to discourage the adventurous from squatting up there.

A young gull dragging a withered leg gazed at us from the roof of one of the many booking kiosks. Maybe it was waiting to go on a boat trip or a fishing expedition to one of the sunken wrecks. Open crabbers and small trawlers rode their moorings in a different world from the candy floss, Pepsi's and fast food you could get over the way. But for those of us who love ale there was the comforting sight of The Crown and Anchor next to The Sprat and Mackerel.

But you have to look to the water for the spirit of Brixham.

The masts of the big trawlers swayed gently in the sky. The fishing fleet "village" lent the town another dimension. Overgang looped up to the left and a band of anglers arrived in a minibus for a day on the sea.

We strolled along the jetty into the smell of salt water. At the end we were surrounded by scrounging gulls and the juvenile birds with their persistent pleas reminded me of the kids I had found begging outside Dublin's Gresham Hotel back in the Fifties and Sixties.

Then the sun peeped over the hill to the south-east and the slanting rays fell on the lifeboat like a spotlight picking out the star of the outer harbour show.

Returning to The Quay with the sun on our shoulders and boats coming to life, we searched for sea dogs and old salts but could only conclude that Sunday early was a bad time for seafarer spotters.

We came past the back of the fisheries museum and the flag poles to the statue of King Billy, a monarch who has had enough publicity elsewhere of late.

On the other side of the road was The Bullers Arms and the Strand Art Gallery placed like a small cultural crown an the head of Carousel Amusements.

The Strand brought us right into Fore Street by the Blue Anchor.

33

"Dug?" Jamie barked. "Sea dog in bunk or snoring in hammock." I said. "Be patient."

He flashed me that "I've been conned" look and proceeded to ignore me.

The first storeys of Fore Street are better than the ground floor development with a few notable exceptions. The Co-op has a fine brick facade dating from 1911 and rising almost apologetically from the awful functional of unlimited plate glass. These big bland display areas are self-defeating. The old shop fronts were elaborate works of art. They offered glimpses of an Aladdin's cave of goods and lured you in to buy.

Most of the shop fronts were identical except for the names above them. Walking Fore Street I realised how we have gutted the homely architecture of yesterday and replaced it with something totally lacking in character and distinction.

The London Inn and The Globe suggested that Brixham was an ideal town for an out-of-season pub crawl and Chandlers Restaurant, with its charming frontage, was an indictment of all we have lost in the pursuit of the characterless.

We were back at Bolton Cross, me and the disappointed terrier. He hadn't seen a pirate, a sea captain, a one-eyed sea cook, a peg-legged buccaneer or any sort of sea dog or salt in thigh boots and navy blue jersey reeking of grog and tar.

"OK I'm sorry," I said unable to meet his gaze.

We came up New Road again and Jamie loosed a happy bark. On the roof of the shop called Second Thoughts was a Highland sheep dog with the long serious face of Lassie.

"Bow wow," Jamie exclaimed. "What did I tell you?" I said smugly. "Where else would you find a dog on a roof?" He shook his head.

Brixham was OK as far as he was concerned.

Walk 13—Part One: Paignton to Waddeton

Distance: four and a half miles (via Galmpton)

I like blending tastes—coming down off Dartmoor after a day alone to the takeaways and pubs of Torbay. Maybe this preference pushed me into doing a little urban and rural classic. Certainly it gave me the chance to get around places where I grew up—a Roots Route if you like.

It was Saturday and my soccer club Paignton Town hadn't selected me for the game at Clennon Valley. Two indifferent first team appearances had merely confirmed that Anno Domini had triumphed over talent! So when the afternoon loomed huge, blank and colourless I decided to take the dog on another nostalgia trail. Apart from the actual joy of walking I'd have an opportunity to visit a few of the old soccer haunts and let some ghosts out to play. The football junkie would get his mild fix.

Jamie the Jack Russell's age in human reckoning is around 77 and he didn't complain when he settled in my big rucksack to be carried most of the way. His head stuck out the top and I'm sure he felt superior to the dogs trotting by.

We set off from the Totnes Road end of Winner Street with rain trying to fall from a grey sky.

Crossing Totnes Road I came swiftly down Fisher Street and passed Grosvenor Terrace and the Torbay Inn en route to the Big Tree. Surely this giant macrocarpa is the most famous landmark in Torbay. It is definitely Paignton's most celebrated

Victorian, a family favourite and Britain's most noble bus stop. My father sat on its bench and my mother continues to do so at the end of her walks. The past won't let us go.

I walked on along Dartmouth Road with Western Close on the site of the old GWR goods yard. Then I was at Penwill Way and the new homes which stand on the gone-forever allotments where my parents grew their vegetables.

Beyond Clennon Valley Leisure Centre were the football pitches. Paignton Town were performing there on the way to a one nil defeat at the hands of Upton Athletic Reserves. My heart was with the lads.

I played the first game for the Town at Clennon after the move from the Green around 1954 when I was 17. I consider it a privilege to have turned out for the club again a few weeks ago at the age of 51 even though it was no Roy of the Rovers hero's return.

I was talking to the dog as I came up the hill to Waterside and the Waterside Hotel which was a favourite haunt of that great Paignton character Donkey Daniels. Once, after a session in the public bar, Mr Daniels tried to take a pony on a doubledecker bus—and for half fare because he claimed the animal was under 14.

The dog and I left the shops and the church and crossed the road to walk the pavement of the mini-dual carriageway. The sea was a dull gleam behind the railway embankment under the little hill called the Sugar Loaf. My dad courted my mam on that hill and my grandad and gran sat on its summer turf. The hometown scene is always alive with bits of family history.

Near the bus shelter where the carriageway ended were the best looking haws I've seen this autumn—big plump red berries next to curls of Old Man's Beard.

I crossed the road again and marched briskly with the dog on my back to Windy Corner. There's an evocative name for you! Here the urban surrenders unwillingly to the rural. I passed the bus shelter and wandered over the common of Galmpton Warborough. Wild flowers were blooming in the grass around the granite war memorial cross raised by the parishioners of Churston Ferrers to the memory of local men killed in the Great War. The dozen names were 12 too many lost in that great ocean of violence and death.

I bounded over the turf and said "Good afternoon" to four women with shopping bags and Devon accents. The shell of the windmill was on the skyline and southwards fields were coming under the plough. Certain aspects of life are apparently changeless. Maybe the little spinney of mainly hawthorns was a fitting monument to the Churston soldiers lost in that distant war.

The villas and bungalows of Galmpton's outskirts brought me back into the present. They had neat lawns and hedges between their unruffled privacy and the traffic din.

The football pitch just up the road could boast something more animated. Galmpton United were drawing 0-0 with St Marychurch Spurs in a South Devon League Premier Division match.

The village club reflects much of what is good and appealing about rural soccer and when I turned into Greenway Road I met one of the game's 24-carat gold personalities—Pam Emmins.

Pam is a Stoke Gabriel woman and the sort of soccer supporter you find in fiction. Many a time over the past four decades she has roared at me and many a time I've roared back.

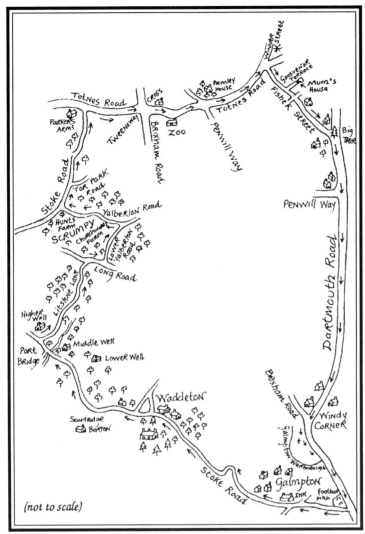

(not to scale)

It was nice to exchange a few pleasantries with her before ambling on down to the fork and bearing left along Stoke Gabriel Road at the Manor Inn which is a good country pub.

Soon Slade Lane was behind me and Galmpton Stores was on the left and I was loitering in front of buildings like Glenside and Park Vale with its attractive verandah. The village jigsaw began to assemble around me—Galmpton Congregational Church facing M. and J. Lees the butchers and the Galleon Stores and Post Office. Horses neighed in nearby fields and the road was narrowing to show off the charms of Poacher's Cottage and Orchard Cottage. The dog stirred in the rucksack as I passed Old Road and a cul-de-sac of modern development called The Orchard. Facing it was a row of clean-cut white houses, one with the bows of a rowing boat as a porch over its front door. Good idiosyncratic stuff, real South Devon village architecture — and so was Ivy Cottage and its off-cream walls and blue paintwork.

A hedgebank was on the right and an ivy clad wall on the left. Beyond the buildings were orchards and ponies. Above them sailed the last of the spent summer's swallows and housemartins.

The dog fidgeted again and I was beginning to think he wanted to cock his leg. I hurried past the converted outbuildings of Manor Farm and the splash of colour in the garden of Lee Cottage to the last dwelling in this part of the village No. 102 Stoke Road.

Then I unslung the rucksack and let out the terrier. He yawned stretched and scratched, eager to be off.

The road looped up a steep hill under tree rustle. A grey wagtail skipped ahead of us and brought us to a halt. This turned out to be lucky for we could look back from the bend to the old village. Presently a gateway obliged with a view over fields to the Dart. On the brow of the hill a lot of mature trees were catching the wind and walking down I could see Windmill Clump, rain-blurred and far off, but still presiding over the frontiers of the Forties childhood.

To the left were flashes of the Dart through the trees of Barn Wood. Pigeons clattered off the plough and close at hand in the hedge were masses of blue-black bullens. I ate a few and gazed at the facade of Waddeton Court on its slope of parkland. Sheep grazed among big conifers below the house but Jamie and I were strolling on between the cider apple orchards into the hamlet of Waddeton.

Part Two: Waddeton to Paignton

Distance five and a half miles (via Port Bridge, Yalberton and Collaton St Mary)

After walking from Paignton along Dartmouth Road to Galmpton the terrier and I took Stoke Road to Waddeton through gentle countryside.

Again it tried to rain, again it failed and around the bend we were greeted by pink cottages with white paintwork under smoke-darkened thatch and everything laid out beneath the deep cawing of the rooks in the tall firs of Waddeton Court.

The big oak stood in the middle of the hamlet where two roads met. The last time I was there was two springs ago when this was part of a route I was doing for a walks book.

It was good to see the faded hydrangeas and pink wash of Tree Cottage facing the pillars of the entrance to Waddeton Court. Jamie and a scruffy work dog sniffed at each other in a friendly fashion before I walked him past the rural development of Waddeton Home Farm and the old grey buildings of East Farm.

A little before we reached the oak on the right the milestone in the wall informed me it was 5 miles to Totnes.

In the days before cars when the working man walked everywhere or scrounged a lift on a wagon, this sort of distance must have been significant. It was for an OAP dog but Jamie wasn't tiring yet.

He trotted up to the inevitable pink Waddeton Pool Cottage and watered the verge. An even older dog than himself slept by the front door and in the paddock at the side were six white geese and a hen with tiny chicks.

It was comforting to know that this was someone's home, a place radiating human warmth.

We left it to enter a world of small fields, trees, red soil and stubble populated by wild creatures and farm animals. I know this landscape well and I love it. There was the wind in the treetops and the buzz of electricity in overhead electricity cables. Autumn was creeping over the countryside.

The drive to Sandridge Barton was conspicuously signposted and above the fields which swept down to the woods and the Dart the sky was suddenly full of rooks. The uncertain greens of the season were turning yellow and bronze but a swallow swooped low in a curve of defiance.

With the turning to Byter Downe Kennels up on the left I preferred to gaze across the coombe to the orchards fields and geese of Lower Well Farm.

Under the trees on the brow of the next hill was another milestone telling me I was four miles from Totnes.

Dog and I wandered down past the entrance to Lower Well and the big notice informing motorists that sacks of spuds could be bought at the farm. Middle Well a bit further on had the air of a residential dwelling determined to remain so.

We crossed Port Bridge over a stream which I first discovered not long after Hitler's War. Now there was a climb to Higher Well Farm where we turned right into what I've always known as Litstone Lane. Here we met a friendly old gentleman and his two elderly workdogs driving four cows.

The hedgebanks had been trimmed. The lane wound between them opening once into a smallholding then running on to the disused quarry and the crag that I climbed often during my boyhood for the kestrel eggs.

At the bend was the thick 15 ft high stump of a tree stripped clean of its bark like a natural totem pole. The stream was on the right and flies lifted in a humming cloud of fresh cowdung.

The tall dark "nave" of hazel bushes ushered us by Whitehill Copse. Vandals had tipped rubbish at the wayside and it angered me to see old gas stoves abandoned among wild flowers.

Jamie stopped and sighed and waited to be rubbed down and returned to the rucksack for a well-earned ride on my back.

With many right-angled turns the lane faltered up the hill, its high hedges hiding the views. And suddenly I was confronted by the vision of Yalberton Industrial Estate up ahead. OK, there has to be some urban expansion but so much of it looks like Hell's suburbs and I lament what we have lost.

I strode into Long Road and came right downhill over the little bridge past the orchards to Lower Yalberton and the left-hand turn into Lower Yalberton Road. Orchards were on both sides and the electricity cables stretched above us to the pylon that towered over the apples trees.

Leaving a row of cottages which stood at the wayside, I looked out across the coombe to the yard of Hunts farm. Nine Acres market garden was at the right hand but the industrial sprawl dominated the foreground.

I turned from it to gaze for a moment down on the pigs penned in Vic Churchward's orchards. The grass was littered with windfalls and I recalled other autumns long ago when I had bagged apples ready for the mill.

Swinging sharp left into Yalberton Road, me and the sleeping dog passed some thatched cottages and went over the bridge to the barn shop where Churchward's Prize Cider is on sale. Having worked for Vic when I was young and him putting up with my ineptitude I know all about the quality of the stuff on offer. I had a sample and came away with a gallon of rough (dry to the respectable) in a plastic container. Lovely agricultural wine!

Up the hill Mr Hunt was also selling good cider at his farm. Certainly Higher Yalberton is the place to go if you have a taste for real Devon farmhouse scrumpy and if you see angels queuing at the barn don't be surprised. Even in Heaven they don't make cider like this.

Up on Stoke Road I bore right and the dog let me know he was ready to walk again. Traffic roared by, but infrequently. Beyond Tor Park Road again on the right the industrial sprawl lay like a menace.

"Do you suppose," I asked the dog "that mess up there will swamp Higher Yalberton some day in the future?"

He grinned like a politician but made no reply.

Countryside finally ended at the Parker's Arms and Totnes Road although climbing the hill to the right we had to pass Collaton Farm. It was there at the wayside, an outpost of another world, a world where the seasons still had relevance.

At the top of the hill Jamie told me he would like to get back in the rucksack. Maybe the urban development opposite Paignton Lower School wasn't to his liking or maybe he really was "bushed".

I walked on over Tweenaway Cross to Paignton Zoo, the past snapping at my heels. Primary school visits to the zoo came poignantly to mind and Primley House in its trees a short distance beyond Waterleat Road, nudged other areas of my past into focus. The Whitleys lived here once and I ran over their estate in the summer holidays of childhood.

Then I was striding down into Paignton's suburbia leaving Merrits Flats behind me, with memories of my mother and me in war-time rooms in Elmbank Raad fading now.

The urban present was taking over and as we reached the traffic lights and Winner Street once more I was thinking of the evening meal and a glass of Churchward's scrumpy to ease the heartache.

Walk 14—The North Whilborough Circular

Distance: One and a half miles (incorporating Compton Mill and Bickley)

This route is a little country road classic, a rural triangle laid around 344 ft Farradon Hill.

The clocks had gone back the night before and the dog and I gloried in the early morning sunlight.

A kind gentleman at the Bickley Mill Inn west of Edginswell let me leave the car in his car park and, as the Jack Russell and I set off, three mute swans passed overhead with a creak of wings. The only other sounds were the singing clatter of a stream and the regular detonations of a crow scarer.

We left the inn bearing right before a left-hand turn brought us up the lane past some little wooden chalets stuck on the hillside.

Trees were shedding their leaves and the banks each side of us carried the clearly defined paths of foxes and badgers. A grey squirrel took one look at Jamie the dog and ran up a telegraph pole.

"So much for canine charisma," I said.

He grinned and winked.

We came into glaring sunlight on the brow of the hill and descended with bowed heads amongst all the puddles and leaf litter. I delighted in the vision of wooded distances and the mooing that carried across the fields. The sun was warm enough to set the gnats dancing above the manure the cattle had deposited on the road.

We walked by the bungalow called Karnten down into the hamlet of North

Whilborough and I was reminded of Sabbath strolls with Gran through the lanes of yesterday's Devon. At the houses we swung right below a tall chimney stack and a starling that was delivering his morning aria.

"Guhhd," Jamie said although birdsong normally leaves him cold.

Beside a cottage door was a sign that read Queen Anns.

Queen Ann's what? I wondered. Nearby a tractor was parked between a van and a car then there was a street lamp in the front garden of Ladysmith Cottages like a prop from a Magritte landscape. The house had a lovely door and a bit of a porch and a late blooming of roses. Sunnyside offered a garden full of begonias and Rose Cottage presented a garden full of bees.

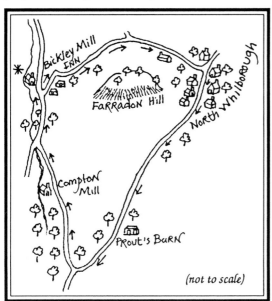

(not to scale)

Everywhere rural dreams were being realised but probably nowhere more emphatically than at Ye Olde Thatched Cottage opposite a touch of Mid-Atlantic development. Whilborough Farmhouse Cottage led logically to Barters Old Farmhouse and Whilborough Farmhouse but the fine stone and tile conversion on the left came as a surprise. Passing Swallows and Cyder Barn with its French-looking courtyard I was beginning to think I had wandered into a chapter from *Wind in the Willows*. Then I found Court Farm with its handsome lawns and shrubs and a red-leaved creeper covering the front of the building. Sheer delight which the terrier saluted on three legs!

We walked up a lane beneath bushy hazels pausing to admire a modest white residence called The Firs. The bale of hay on the back of the parked tractor hinted at genuine agricultural goings on but Barters Farm is a large modern bungalow which might put off a rural romantic in pursuit of one of those corners of Whimshire where the cows never drop steaming dollops and even the sheep have light lounge bar accents.

North Whilborough has a charm of its own, a quiet vitality many a showpiece Cotswold village lacks. But it was behind us now and I was stopping at a metal gate under the buzz of electricity cables to gaze across the field to a view of houses on a hillside beyond a shallow coombe.

Strolling on I was confronted by one of those visions of small fields and the gleam of red soil that was so Devon it balled the emotion in my throat. Sunlight lent the plough a flush and heightened the autumn colours in the trees.

We passed Prout's Barn which looks as if it is being converted into a stable block and came down to the crossroads to turn right above a tree-choked coombe. The sun flashed and winked on wet leaves and a brook rushed through the meadows masked by foliage. Up on the skyline to the right was the silhouette of a ruined windmill but in the coombe the leaves of the scrub willow were whitening in the wind and we were suddenly at Compton Mill and its pig pens. A little further down the lane a sun-drenched beech and horse chestnut were wearing their October beauty and I halted to take it in.

Presently we crossed a small bridge over a small Devon stream to Bickley Mill Cross where we took the Kingskerswell road and walked right. Jamie waded through the drifts of dead leaves and I picked up a few windfalls dropped by the cider apple trees of the orchard at the wayside.

Beyond the next bend was Bickley Mill Inn again and Jamie had forgotten to fake weariness. He had the air of a pup as he drank his water and crunched a handful of cat biscuits.

We brought our happiness back to the breakfast table.

Walk 15—To Sugar Loaf Hill and Broadsands

Distance: about one and a quarter miles

Thursday morning began with a light fall of drizzle but the sky was brightening as the dog and I left the car just down from the house called The Stoep at the top of Waterside Road.

The recent fine spell had spoilt my Jack Russell and he blinked and frowned as the rain ghosted around him.

But he resigned himself to a drenching and I led him back into Broadsands Park Road to walk left, downhill past shrubby, conifery gardens and substantial houses.

Among the fallen leaves, rain-pasted to the pavements, were scatterings of haws.

Jamie shook himself and looked up. Blue patches were appearing among the clouds.

"That's better," I said, remembering the surfeit of H_2O we endured back in the summer.

Where the road swung left opposite Broadsands Avenue we were confronted by Broadsands Viaduct and a tall tree with a crow's nest in its top branches. It was pleasant to stand before the elegant stone arches. Elegance is rare in much of today's functional architecture.

"Ready?" I asked the terrier.

"Furr whutt?" he barked.

"The steps," I said from a demoniacal grin.

And we came left up the flight which is part of the Coastal Footpath.

Jamie took them in a series of little jumps which wasn't bad at all for a dog with short legs.

Next to the 65th was a bench that we didn't use and before long we had done the entire 120 steps to stand on the grassy knoll. The sun came out and the rain stopped and I could enjoy the splendid view south over Broadsands, to Churston Point and Berry Head.

Among the grass were plenty of seeding plants to tempt goldfinches and we were privileged to see a small "charm" of these beautifully coloured little birds feasting on the burrs and thistleheads.

Leaving the knoll we crossed a meadow towards a view of Hope's Nose, Thatcher

41

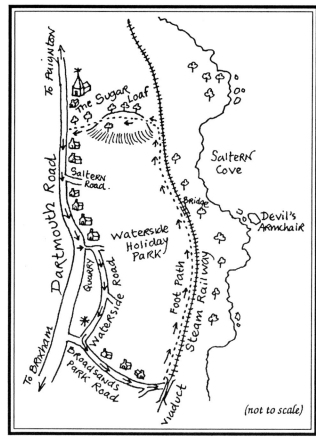

To Paignton

The Sugar Loaf

Saltern Road.

Dartmouth Road

Quarry

Waterside Road

To Brixham

Broadsands Park Road

Viaduct

Saltern Cove

Bridge

Devil's Armchair

Waterside Holiday Park

Foot Path

Steam Railway

(not to scale)

Rock and Orestone. A couple of rabbits hopped out of the railway embankment brambles, saw Jamie and hopped back again.

"You have this devastating effect on four-legged wildlife," I said, and he looked away and sniffed.

The meadow ended and we trudged up a narrow muddy footpath with garden fences and hedges to the left and bramble and bracken thickets on the other side.

A bench near the end of the path was strategically situated. About ten paces further on was a steep flight of steps and old folk reversing this walk may be glad of a rest after tackling this stretch.

The dog went down the steps with a nimbleness you don't normally expect from an old age pensioner.

The rock called Devil's Armchair was below the cliffs to the right and ranks of caravans stood on the left. Then a small flight of steps brought us on past the railway bridge towards the Sugar Loaf and more steps.

The terrier sighed.

Counting the newest addition there are 79 steps but the council workmen have placed a bench alongside the 46th.

"A nice gesture, James," I said.

But he was concentrating.

On the grassy dome of Sugar Loaf he rested while I enjoyed a bird's eye view of Paignton over its gleaming rooftops. It was a moving experience. My grandparents and parents had stood on that little hill staring across the bay to Torquay or letting their eyes wander to the sandstone tower of the parish church.

There would have been more green spaces in those days but the small fields, bounded by wild hedges on the landward side of Sugar Loaf, probably hadn't

42

changed much over the years.

Surprisingly, the dog didn't demand to be carried. He walked beside me over the field, taking in the smells, and we negotiated the gap in the hedge with the help of three log-edged steps cut in the mud.

Another tiny unkempt field saw us down to the pavement and Dartmouth Road. Bearing left we strolled beside gardens and bungalows, past Saltern Road, to the telephone kiosk at the entrance to Waterside Holiday Park.

Then we went down the little ramp and swung sharp right into Waterside Road.

Walking up the hill with the old foxy quarry on the right, I could look over the caravan-choked coombe to the Sugar Loaf—that lovely little hill of my childhood.

On the wall above the caravan park there were the tiny delicate flowers of hundreds and thousands, and valerian in bloom.

"Tired?" I asked the dog as we tramped round the bend flanked by tall, tree-clad banks.

"Nuhh," he grunted.

Leaves fell and danced in the air around us and there was more blue sky now than grey.

Walk 16—Odicknoll to South Whilborough and back

Distance: One mile and a bit

A little after sunrise I drove from Edginswell towards Kingskerswell under Hamelin Way to park in the lane on the left with just a glimpse of Odicknoll Farm a little further up.

It was a still, frosty morning and white sheep stood motionless in whiter fields. The sky was thrush egg blue, the sun low and glazing everything it touched with frail gold.

"A morning designed for pre-Raphaelite poets," I informed the terrier. He nodded and cocked his leg.

At first, because of the frost powder on the road, he was reluctant to set his feet down but he soon warmed to the business as we loped off Kingskerswell way in the direction of Little Cuthill and Cleveland.

The wayside notice informed us that organically grown vegetables were available at Odicknoll.

"Wurf," Jamie said.

The plant-life on the verges was still and white.

"Why can't it be like this at Christmas?" I said.

"Duh nuh," the dog replied.

The continuous roar of traffic lifted from the A380 Newton Abbot road a few fields away. To our left was a big hump of furze-hackled downland which probably has a local name but is nameless on the Ordnance Survey map.

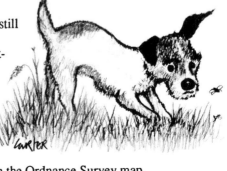

We strode briskly past Ganders Park and its residential mobile homes with Applegarth and Home Park to the left.

It was an odd little tucked away corner of South Devon constantly threatened, I suppose, by Torbay's urban expansion. That's a pity.

The dwelling called Little Mead was very Californian—lawns, palms, pool and a kind of colonial Spanish architecture which I liked.

A flail mower had been over the hedges, roughing them up, but better now, at year's end than in the spring.

Birds sat silently in bare top boughs and I was presented with a gateway view of the traffic crawling along the main road to Torquay. In the distance was the spire of the Roman Catholic Church at St Marychurch and the magic of frostfire lay on everything.

Just before Stokeleigh Farm we bore left and came up the lane past stables and

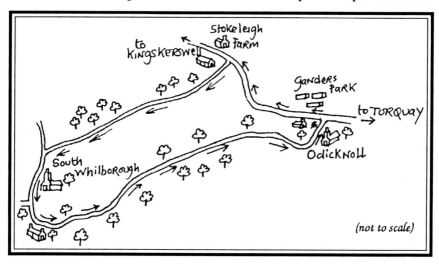

horses. The hedges were high and so were our spirits for all creatures respond to fine weather.

The dog stopped on the brow of the hill and while he scratched I looked back to Torquay's towers and spires. The nameless hill was wreathed in sun-smoke and brown cattle lounged about on white pasture. To the right was a bit of orchard.

These small rural backwaters must remain rural. The air was crisp and the quiet beauty of the morning prevailed. Then I found a dead shrew lying frost-rimed on the frozen mud and laid him to rest in the hedgetop. To get killed by a car in that lonely place didn't seem right. In any case, the discovery of a small life snuffed out amid all the glory of late autumn was sad.

Sensing my melancholy the dog looked up at me, whining his concern. I patted him and we walked on.

Down in the coombe ahead were the outbuildings of South Whilborough and a glimpse of steaming thatch. We were pacing over frozen mud which held the imprints of horses' hooves when Jamie suddenly stopped, his ears erect. From the hedge came a patter as if lots of tiny animals were on the move. But it was leaves unhooking and falling and brushing against other leaves on their way to the bottom of the hedge.

Farm noises swelled to greet us and we came to South Whilborough with its lovely yard and equally fine thatched house dominated by a tall chimney. It was good to be among orchards and stroll on up a hill any octogenarian dwarf could tackle with ease after a night on the scrumpy.

A pair of thatched cottages stood together on the bend—one mustard coloured, the other pink. Beyond them, on the left, was the shock of a coal yard and its rickety corrugated buildings. But at the right hand side was the consolation of that high furze-tufted downland and some of Kingskerswell's houses down below in the coombe opposite.

The dog slowed and I looked at him suspiciously.

"My hands are cold," I said. "Do I really have to carry you."

"Nuhh," he snuffled, placing his nose to a dead stoat. The slender creature was warm and unmarked and the cause of its death mystified me. Maybe it had met something bigger than itself and had a heart attack, or maybe old age had finished it off.

I saluted it and gave it an Indian burial.

Then the terrier and I marched down towards the traffic thunder and Odicknoll where contented fowls were banjoing in the yard.

Pausing at the farm gate, me and the lack Russell did the soft shoe shuffle to the birds' gentle jazz.

Walk 17—Conneybear Lane and back to Coffinswell

Distance: one and a half miles

George Sykes, mine host of the Linny Inn, Coffinswell, let me leave my car in his car park and the terrier and I set off into another of those frosty sunlit mornings I can never take for granted.

Leaving the car park we bore right past a row of neat houses and looking back I saw the Linny's thatch steaming in the sun. Frost was also turning to smoke on the thatch of Orchard Way as we came sharp right into Conneybear lane with pleasant dwellings at either hand.

Starlings were taking the sun in the naked apple trees and dogs were barking in the kennels further up the hill. Frost-dusted hedges and plenty of conifers hid courtyards and large gardens. Beyond these comfortable residences the fields wore the glitter of a landscape that was breaking free of frost and ice.

Village suburbia slowly gave way to the agricultural—pasture, root crops, a hilltop spinney. Then through a gap in the hedge on the left I gazed across mist-filled coombes to distant Dartmoor.

Between Coffinswell and that vision of high wilderness were several villages and hamlets lying under smoke from the cottage chimneys.

"Concentrate on the walking," I told Jamie as we sauntered past Aslands Boarding Kennels and the terrier responded to the calls of the inmates.

The outlying houses ended at a copse and we walked beneath lofty oaks whose top boughs were sheathed in sunlight. Someone had built a Tarzan house in a smaller tree. It was surrounded by ropes and rough timber ladders.

"Tarzan, Jane and the chattering chimp," I mumbled remembering the Johnny Weismuller films of my childhood.

"Cheetuh," said the dog who had also seen the Tarzan movies.

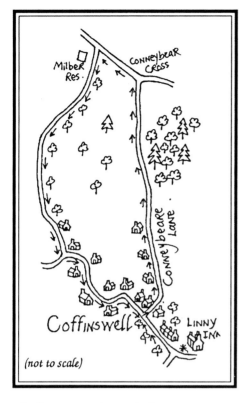

Then we were among open fields and I could look over the left hand hedge across countryside that was as lovely as Eden on the First Morning. The calm was miraculous. Maybe every living creature in South Devon was holding its breath.

The narrow country road ended at Conneybear Cross and a busier road carrying two-way traffic. We turned left here and walked in the direction of Milber, passing a row of stately beeches over on the right which screened views towards Coombein-teignhead and Bishopsteignton.

The passing cars distressed Jamie and both the dog and I thankfully swung sharp left at Milber Reservoir into that soothing rustic quietude and incredible view. The muted colours of the season, the low mist and the low hills and their copses swam into haze at the bottom of the sky.

In the east, above the sea, was a bank of innocent clouds. Smoke rose from chimneys and sheep grazed the hush. The scene possessed the quality of a fine watercolour painting.

"Nuhss," said the terrier.

"Better than nice," I said. "Marvellous."

"Muh-vuh-luss," he barked.

The sun was warm on my face and like the dog, I was feeling cheerful and ready for anything.

Three or four magpies dipped over the hedge and flew chattering into the orchard. The lowing of cattle fed the morning's unblemished peacefulness. It was amazing— there on the doorstep of Torbay with all its noise and bustle, a part of the universe in which Old Billy Blake and Wordsworth could have felt at home.

We came left with the bend although the option to go right availed itself.

Beyond Manor Farm leaves were making a slow descent through shafts of sunlight and marching past Rock Cottage we found ourselves in the bottom of Coffinswell. A cock crowed over the white thatch of the shadowy, frost-bound coombe and cars on nearby parking lots were showing a reluctance to start.

The mist streaming off the thatched roofs was full of the sun and Coffinswell is thatched, with noticeable exceptions, from end to end.

The dog and I followed the road through the village back to the Linny Inn where George kindly offered me tea. Alas, I was bound for Torbay but some of the morning's calm travelled with me.

46

Walk 18—Barton Pines and Lower Blagdon

Distance: about 3 miles

The proprietor of the pleasant little hilltop inn, Barton Pines, told me it would be OK to leave the car in his car park.

The morning was beautiful after the previous day's heavy rain and the dog and I said goodbye to the Barton Pines' peacocks and strolled into it.

Rooks in the tree tops loosed their caws after us as we bore right down the hill. It was the last day of November and there was a hint of Christmas in the air. While Jamie picked his way through the leaf mush I gazed over the fields to Tor Bay and Berry Head. I was in one of those familiar boyhood places under the great oaks, remembering Sunday afternoon walks with my parents.

On the left a trickle of a stream ran alongside the hedge and the Jack Russell and I were descending into a countryside of small copses, orchards and coombes. Smoke climbed lazily from chimneys and we came past Higher Blagdon with Peach Cottage standing beneath its thatch on the right and the farm facing it.

The sun was warm.

We came down between ferny banks to Blagdon House. In the orchards a few crimson cider apples still clung to the branches and it was good to be there in South Devon walking a country road under a blue sky and bird calls.

At Blagdon House we swung left into Lower Blagdon and ambled down the lane with old and new farm buildings at either hand. Sparrows pursued us and I took out a stale bun and crumbled it for them.

The coombe was dotted with dwellings but one particularly fine example of rural development in rough sandstone called Old Barn House caught the eye. Behind it was a pleasant mustard-coloured country house with silver birches in its garden.

We came past Orchard Cottage and up the hill to swing right beyond the stand of firs. Winter thrushes deserted the hedges to fan out over the meadows. On the brow of the hill I looked back to Barton Pines and saw the clouds sailing in from the west.

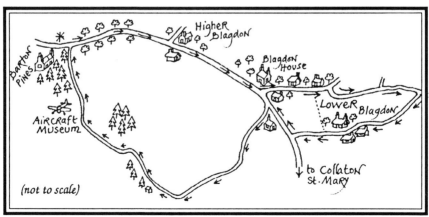

The dog and I sniffed the air before pacing down the lane towards Paignton's housing estate suburbs. Then we took the sharp right turn into a lane guarded by well-trimmed hedges. More cloud drifted over the sky.

"Rain?" I said.

"Purhh-hupps," Jamie snuffled leading me up to the next hilltop and a glimpse across the coombe of the busy main Totnes road. Where the way looped on down, a stately beech was conspicuous among less elegant hedgerow trees.

Then dark thatch announced the outlying cottages of Lower Blagdon. A nice old house stood in its gardens behind high stone walls to the right and there was the walnut tree that yielded so many nuts in the golden scrumping days of my childhood.

A grey wagtail bobbed about by the brook and the footpath and a crow sat languidly in the jagged top boughs of a big tree that had been struck by lightning.

The dog and I walked up the lane towards the ghost of half a moon beneath flocks of thrushes and finches. Despite my intimacy with the place, these little corners and coombes at the back of Torbay never fail to delight me.

Presently we were on the Collaton St Mary-Barton Pines road again, bearing right between an orchard and a high wall. Just before we reached the barn at the top of the orchard we turned left and walked out of Lower Blagdon.

A bank of cloud was rolling in and coming to the top of the rise I could gaze up

at Windmill Clump on the horizon beyond the Totnes road. For a moment I felt the approaching rain was stalking me. Traffic din disturbed the calm but the dog and I were moving briskly down beneath hazel hedges to a lin-hay and a group of firs. A grey squirrel ran across the lane in front of us and Jamie was instantly leaping about on the end of his lead.

"Canine capers?" I murmured, when he had settled again.

We had enjoyed the best of the day and I was happy as we sauntered along beside a stream which was half lost in vegetation. Up on the hill ahead was a larch plantation and rounding the next bend we met the sound of running water.

"Tired?" I asked Jamie as we contemplated the final leaf strewn ascent.

"Nuhh," he said.

A buzzard lifted and flapped away off the sheep pasture. The hill was steep but although he was puffing a bit the terrier managed it without complaint. Wood pigeons and magpies flew away whenever we passed a gate and could be seen from the open fields.

Despite his apparent nonchalance it must have been a relief for Jamie when the way levelled out and we strolled past The Aircraft Museum. The World War Two planes stranded in the late 1980s on the Devon hill were slightly bizarre. Many locals will regret the closure of this out-of-the-way tourist attraction.

But the cawing of rooks in the pines was comforting and to the right lay that remarkable vision of Tor Bay. Rural repose prevailed and returning to my starting place I was pleased to find some of my childhood world still intact.